Centering
Epistemic Injustice

Centering Epistemic Injustice

Epistemic Labor, Willful Ignorance, and Knowing Across Hermeneutical Divides

Kamili Posey

LEXINGTON BOOKS
Lanham • Boulder • New York • London

Published by Lexington Books

An imprint of The Rowman & Littlefield Publishing Group, Inc.
4501 Forbes Boulevard, Suite 200, Lanham, Maryland 20706
www.rowman.com
6 Tinworth Street, London SE11 5AL, United Kingdom

British Library Cataloguing in Publication Information Available

Library of Congress Cataloging-in-Publication Data

Names: Posey, Kamili, author.
Title: Centering epistemic injustice : epistemic labor, willful ignorance,
    and knowing across hermeneutical divides / Kamili Posey.
Description: Lanham : Lexington Books, 2021. | Includes bibliographical
    references and index. | Summary: "Centering Epistemic Injustice asks
    what it means for accounts of epistemic injustice to take seriously the
    lives and perspectives of socially marginalized knowers and the
    strategies that marginalized knowers use to circumvent persistent
    testimonial injustice"-- Provided by publisher.
Identifiers: LCCN 2021020614 (print) | LCCN 2021020615 (ebook) | ISBN
    9781498572576 (cloth) | ISBN 9781498572583 (ebook)
Subjects: LCSH: Justice (Philosophy) | Knowledge, Theory of. | Marginality,
    Social.
Classification: LCC B105.J87 P67 2021 (print) | LCC B105.J87 (ebook) |
    DDC 172/.2--dc23
LC record available at https://lccn.loc.gov/2021020614
LC ebook record available at https://lccn.loc.gov/2021020615

To the streets of New York City and those who walk them with me.

Contents

Introduction

Between me and the other world there is ever an unasked question: unasked by some through feelings of delicacy; by others through the difficulty of rightly framing it. All, nevertheless, flutter around it . . . How does it feel to be a problem? I answer seldom a word.

—W. E. B. Du Bois (1903)

"Could it be that we matter?" asked Black Lives Matter co-founder Patrisse Cullors as she drove around Ferguson in the aftermath of the fatal police shooting of Michael Brown (2017, 213). Could it be that *Black* lives matter? Cullors and Asha Bandele felt a different atmosphere growing in Ferguson than what they felt in Sanford, Florida when Trayvon Martin was killed in 2012. Protesters filled the streets wearing photos of Brown on T-shirts and were carrying signs in support of the prosecution of Darren Wilson. *Could it be that we matter?* What was different about Ferguson? "Trayvon Martin was killed in a gated community," Cullors and Bandele write in *When They Call You a Terrorist: A Black Lives Matter Memoir*, "a place where people do not have the same familial relations with one another, a place intended to separate people, section them off" (2017, 213). The grief and pain felt in Ferguson felt different because that grief was shared, because it was understood by the community. One need not be Black to share in the pain of Black death but there is something about being Black that makes that pain acutely understood. When Eric Garner, Elijah McClain, Manuel Ellis, George Floyd, and other Black bodies cried, "I can't breathe," at the hands of police, what exactly was understood and what exactly was *misunderstood*? Speech originating from undesirable bodies is often, in turn, deemed undesirable. *I can't breathe*. How could a plea be more explicit? What mechanisms interrupt the epistemic uptake of such a distressing claim? To whom speech is aimed matters a great deal. Outside of communities that share our history, marginalized knowers find that we must work to be heard, and sometimes, when we are most in need, we are not heard at all. There is an intricate and unstable relationship between identity and testimony that unjustly impacts how we come to be understood in the wider social world.

Undesired speech hinges to bodies marked by prejudice, finding that that speech is "unable to do the things [we] intend and expect it to do" (McKinney 2016, 263). Marginalized speech exists on shaky ground between the speech itself and the social and political context surrounding that speech. More often than not, these social and political contexts are rooted in long histories of violence and oppression. Marginalized knowers are compelled to engage in an epistemic dance where we desire to represent our beliefs accurately while also anticipating what socially dominant knowers will believe *about* our speech. To borrow from W. E. B. Du Bois, social marginalization cultivates a kind of *double-consciousness*, or double-knowing. We must know ourselves as both individuals and as our perceived stereotypes, as epistemic agents in our own right, and as epistemic ciphers ready to stand-in for whatever stereotype operates upon us. Misjudging the social and political context in which we find ourselves, or thinking only through our own epistemic lens, can lead to dangerous real-life consequences. In societies bifurcated by hierarchies of dominance and oppression, as in the case of white dominance and Black oppression, the world is translated into one of *subject* and *object*. By social power alone, dominant subjects reconstruct marginalized subjects as social objects—objects to study, control, use, and manipulate. Subjects have the power to dictate what constitutes a social problem while objects are conceived of *as* the social problem.

Double-consciousness arises from the necessity to see oneself according to this perverse distinction. This is not because it is an ontologically accurate distinction, or because it is just, or redeemable in any way, but because without such an understanding we face both social and epistemic risk. When Du Bois gives voice to the unasked question—*How does it feel to be a problem?*—he is a subject compelled to recognize his objectness in the eyes of dominant others. When marginalized knowers find that our speech or testimony cannot do what we want or need it to do in the wider social world, we also come face-to-face with our own objectness. We are negative stereotypes, holders of identity prejudice, vessels on to which the social anxieties of dominant others are placed. If this is the perception of marginalized knowers, as objects without agency, then we can more easily explain why our cries for help and pleas for mercy are not heard. But—and to be clear—we are not, and never were, objects without agency. This is what I take to be behind Du Bois's paradoxical response, "I answer seldom a word." For subjects consider questions but objects do not answer. In what follows, I aim to rethink undesired speech by undesirable bodies, failed uptake, and motivated ignorance in terms of epistemic injustice and the epistemic labor marginalized knowers are compelled to do in hostile and radically unjust epistemic environments. I invoke Du Bois's concept of double-consciousness, or *double-knowing*, as a way of distancing myself from predominant views of epistemic injustice that theorize marginalized knowers as epistemic objects on to which dominant prejudices and anxieties are actualized, rendering marginalized knowers as solely victims of unjust objectification, with minimal agency or resistance strategies for the injustice that we face.

This is project also aims to problematize epistemic remedies for epistemic injustice that fail to address underlying social inequities, pulling apart epistemic power from social power in ways that only superficially resolve epistemic problems, leaving social and political problems woefully intact. Thinking through the work of Linda Martín Alcoff, Patricia Hill Collins, José Medina, Gaile Pohlhaus, Jr., and others, I consider how social power and the desire to protect positions of social dominance influences what dominant knowers are willing to know about marginalized knowers and marginalized epistemic resources. Such discussions tend to naturally wade into social psychological waters, asking what it means to willfully *not know*, or to willfully avoid knowing things that challenge the dominant status quo. I aim to rethink some of the literature that suggests that dominant knowers can intervene into the operations of their nonconscious prejudices and to challenge the idea that bias and prejudice can easily be trained away. There are no easy answers to these issues. Like current debates about whiteness and white privilege, much of what upholds the frameworks that naturalize epistemic injustice lie in the hands of those who are least likely to investigate those frameworks. When they do investigate the frameworks, they often begin as subjects trying to peer through the glass at curious objects, replicating the oppressive realities that they are trying so hard to understand, and circumscribing the possibility for real revolutionary change.

Epistemic injustice aims to describe a family of epistemic phenomena where knowers are wronged in their capacity as knowers (Fricker 2007, 20). Miranda Fricker's 2007 publication of *Epistemic Injustice: Power and the Ethics of Knowing* ignited a discussion about epistemic injustice and epistemic inequality that finds its roots in the work of Sojourner Truth, Mary Church Terrell, Fannie Barrier Williams, Anna Julia Cooper, Helen Appo Cook, and many others. Fricker does not identify a new phenomenon so much as she adds to an already rich historical discussion concerning epistemic inequality. When Patricia Hill Collins writes of Black women's experiences being "outsiders within" due to occupying social positions that are marginalized on two fronts, non-whiteness and non-maleness, she also claims that the power asymmetry that produces "Black female outsider within status" is of unique social and epistemic value (1986, 15). Epistemic values such as "outsider within" status are undertheorized in current discussions of epistemic injustice and are too often focused on the perspectives of dominantly situated knowers The contention of this project is the idea that epistemic injustice is not *merely* a collection of wrongs and harms perpetrated by dominant knowers against marginalized knowers. Epistemic injustice also involves the myriad ways in which marginalized knowers survive, thrive, and epistemically resist dominant knowing in the face of rampant social and epistemic injustice.

I do not suggest that this project can capture every aspect or position of marginalized knowing. However, I do suggest that because most discussions of epistemic injustice have failed to adequately theorize the epistemic practices marginalized knowers use in the face of epistemic injustice, that there are holes, or *problematics*, in our understanding epistemic injustice. The core concern of this book is to outline the burden of *double-knowing* as it relates to epistemic injustice and to explore how marginalized knowers use double-knowing to navigate explicitly and implicitly hostile epistemic environments. Epistemically hostile environments do not necessarily appear to be so from the outside or as considered from the perspective of dominant knowing. For marginalized knowers, hostile epistemic environments run through much of our everyday social experiences and can be more commonplace than not. Consider the following real-life experiences of Black Americans going about their daily lives. Thanks to social media, these situations are all too familiar, a Black person is engaged in some mundane activity and is approached by a white civilian or white police officer with suspicion for one of the following:

1. Going swimming
2. Shopping in a store
3. Entering our own house or apartment building
4. Driving
5. Playing in a park
6. Sitting in a Starbucks
7. Taking a nap in our dorm lounge
8. Checking out of an Airbnb
9. Campaigning door-to-door
10. Bird-watching

Although these experiences do not belong to Black America alone, the tenor and tone of accusations of wrongdoing in the face of ordinary activities are infected by implicit and explicit race-based attitudes and prejudices. Such prejudices are often experienced by other intersectionally marginalized groups as well. For example, consider a case that occurred at a small Northeast college:

> A transgender student notices that there has been no toilet paper, soap, or paper towels refills in the gender neutral restrooms for 17 days in a row. The student reports the condition to the buildings and grounds department at the college and is told the following: "You must be exaggerating. I've known the guy who services the facilities here for years and he would never do a thing like that. People like you are always stirring things up." The student responds: "Maybe I'm wrong about the number of days, sorry. But is it possible for someone to take a look at it?" The representative consents and the student is waved away from the department.

Fricker describes epistemic injustice as taking two related forms: testimonial injustice and hermeneutical injustice. *Testimonial injustice* occurs when a hearer downgrades the credibility of a speaker due to an identity-based prejudice. *Hermeneutical injustice* occurs when a knower is unable to understand significant aspects of their social experiences due to a structural prejudice in shared or collective hermeneutical resources. If we go back to the above case involving the student, we might interpret it as a paradigmatic case of testimonial injustice. The student was considered to have deflated or diminished credibility in their reporting of the bathroom conditions—despite their being in a position to know—due to an identity-based prejudicial stereotype held by the buildings and grounds worker. This framework for understanding injustice in the transmission of knowledge is a good one. However, what is left out of this analysis by omitting the perspective of and response given by the student? What choices did the student feel free to make during this interaction? How were the student's communicative choices impacted by their recognition of the representative's explicit dismissal of the situation due to identity prejudice?

Upon having their claim met with hostility, the student immediately backpedals and deflates their own credibility in the face of a prejudiced rejection ("Maybe I'm wrong about the number of days, sorry"). The student explicitly minimizes themselves as a knower in order to minimize the impact of the negative stereotype that is operating upon them. For marginalized knowers, this is a familiar story. We learn to soften our voices, to ask questions instead of making statements, and to show passivity and deference in order to achieve the social and epistemic goals that dominant knowers achieve mostly without issue. That is, we learn to work within the parameters of negative stereotypes and to restructure our beliefs in light of any evidence that we will not be heard or believed. As far as I can see it, the account of testimonial injustice offered by Fricker cannot account for this additional epistemic labor. In fact, in Fricker's view, the weight of producing a just testimonial exchange is placed on the dominant hearer who is prejudicially deflating the marginalized speaker's testimony, asking, instead, that the hearer extend or inflate credibility as a corrective measure. This does not allow a marginalized speaker's testimony to be heard *as it is* but as the dominant hearer wrongly filters and downgrades it or wrongly filters it and upgrades it. It is still a harm to marginalized epistemic selfhood that injures the development and deployment of our true epistemic selves.

The harms of epistemic selfhood described here are relational harms. They are created in social and epistemic relationships of dominance and oppression and are thus wholly contextual. This means that marginalized knowers who are able to suitably distance themselves from relations of social dominance (and contexts where social dominance is the status quo) may not be harmed in terms of the development of their epistemic selves. It also means that toxic social and epistemic relationships of dominance only contingently hinder the full realization of epistemic selfhood. Although I consider epistemic selfhood to be a critical component of personhood, epistemic selfhood is not equivalent to personhood. Harms to an epistemic self are not equivalent to harms to personhood. I make this distinction because it is tempting for those theorizing the harms of epistemic injustice from the dominant perspective to overstate the role of social power on the psychic development of marginalized personhood. These interpretations seem to insist on the ability of dominant knowers to reduce marginalized knowers to objects, non-agents, and *non-people*. If this were the case, then the harms of epistemic injustice would indeed be dire, but this argument rests on a specious premise. It rests on the premise that the recognition of marginalized knowers as knowers, or as *people capable of knowing*, is dependent on the social and epistemic sanctioning of those with social power. This is a troubling claim for many reasons but primarily because it denies agency to marginalized knowers and further entrenches the idea that epistemic injustice consists solely in what dominant knowers are *doing to* marginalized knowers.

There is more to achieving epistemic justice than amending unjust credibility deficits and "allowing" marginalized knowers the status of knowers or credible testifiers. A critical part of justice involves recognizing and amending for the harm that injustice causes to those who do not have the power to avoid it. It is also involves accounting for the various ways in which marginalized knowers use our own agency to mitigate the real-world problems and harms caused by constant exposure to epistemic injustice. In Chapter 1, I consider Fricker's argument of testimonial virtue as an epistemic practice to mitigate the impact of testimonial injustice. In her account, the dominant hearer is responsible for cultivating testimonial virtues in order to mitigate unjust deflations of a marginalized speaker's credibility. I argue, however, that testimonial virtue is only a partial solution for dealing with testimonial injustice. This is because it only satisfies the part of an unjust testimonial exchange that pertains to the activities of the dominant hearer and entirely ignores the ways in which marginalized knowers communicate and justify our beliefs in hostile epistemic environments, i.e., it addresses their unjust credibility deflations but not the epistemic labor that unjust credibility deflations elicit from marginalized knowers. As such, it leaves a critical part of the injustice part of epistemic injustice undertheorized.

Social inequality begets epistemic inequality in more ways than by producing persistent credibility deficits and gaps in understanding. In cases where social inequality is the result of long histories of violence and oppression, the epistemic landscape comes to be defined by those histories. Consider a general framework of social inequality that produces a subsequent epistemic inequality:

> Group A has a history of using violence against Group B because they believe Group A to be inferior. Group B begins to anticipate the violence from Group A and develops epistemic strategies to mitigate the impact of violence at the hands of Group A, such as to participate in Group A's belief of their own social superiority despite the violence. Over time, members of Group B develop both social and epistemic stress responses to their interactions with members of Group A (i.e., epistemic stress responses include testimonies generated under duress and in order to satisfy non-epistemic goals, such as the avoidance of violence, and/ or testimonies that explicitly ignore types of evidence deemed noncredible by Group A), as well as epistemic stress responses to forming independent beliefs about themselves and other members of Group B (i.e., one can imagine that it would be difficult but not impossible to form true beliefs about oneself under these conditions).

Even in the event that Group A—by some means of social-epistemic enlightenment—comes to reevaluate their interactions with Group B and opts to abstain from violence against Group B on virtuous grounds, members of Group B may still believe themselves to be in danger when engaging with Group A. Members of Group B *may still be* in very real danger when there is a failure of virtue on the part of members of Group A. Although Group A may now use a framework of virtue for interacting with Group B on most occasions, it may still be unreasonable to assume that these interactions have risen to the level of justice. Group A may correct for their violent and oppressive past but epistemic injustice may continue to persist. This is because Group A has done nothing to amend or atone for the epistemic labor that Group B did, and may continue to do, in order to mitigate violence at the hands of Group A, or for the historical harm done to Group B in terms of their development as knowers in their own right. What is missing is a context for accounting for Group B's *double-knowing* and a way to correct for the *historical epistemic injustice* that has polluted the entire landscape of knowing. To make a blunt parallel, the historical trauma of racism does not go away simply because the racist decides to be less racist, or even anti-racist. This is because the racist has left in his wake a social world that has been defined by and shaped by his problematic beliefs and behaviors.

Furthermore, as the epistemic landscape has been shaped by histories of social and epistemic domination, dominant knowers must learn to untangle their implicit beliefs about marginalized knowers from their explicitly prejudicial past behaviors. Thus, also in chapter 1, I consider the issue of overcoming implicit identity-based biases and prejudices. Fricker argues that dominant knowers can reflect on their conscious activities and "shift intellectual gear out of spontaneous, unreflective [reflection] and into active critical reflection in order to identify how far the suspected prejudice has influenced her judgment" (2007, 91). The claim is that a "fully virtuous" dominant hearer will be so sufficiently conditioned in the ways of epistemic virtue that they can reliably correct their erroneous credibility judgments. Over time, and through exposure to a wide range of experiences, the dominant knower will have so internalized the application of corrective epistemic virtues that their ability to correct themselves in the face of an erroneous credibility judgment will become second nature (Fricker 2007, 97). Like having an epistemic reflex against identity prejudice, the dominant knower becomes something that they previously could not be: a knower who can transcend their social environment and make spontaneous judgments without implicit or explicit bias and prejudice.

However, and even in the best case scenario, dominant knowers who aim to internalize epistemic virtue as a remedy for epistemic injustice will still have to contend with the issue of implicit bias and prejudice. Even if we grant Fricker's claim that synchronic reflexive judgments are possible, is it possible for dominant hearers to maintain this reflexivity consistently over time? I argue that testimonial virtue is not likely to be diachronic in this way. If testimonial virtue is not sufficiently diachronic, and we cannot expect dominant knowers to make consistently virtuous judgments over time, then it is unclear that dominant knowers would ever be habituated toward epistemically virtuous behavior in the sense that Fricker intends. That is, what Fricker requires a virtuous hearer to operationalize will often be beyond their cognitive reach. Similar to other critiques of virtue-based ethics, e.g., the Situationist Challenge, there will always be cases where real-world pressures lead dominant knowers to fail to be epistemically virtuous. This is further complicated by recent evidence that most knowers better learn negative biases, prejudices, and stereotypes, suggesting that negative identity associations are more "cognitively sticky" than positive identity associations. This means that dominant knowers who aim to operationalize epistemic virtue are met with another cognitive roadblock in terms of consistently employing virtue.

Chapter 2 aims to define the concepts of epistemic labor and epistemic burden. Marginalized knowers are often aware of the negative prejudicial lens through which we are viewed as this is the primary feature of double-knowing. In many instances, we are compelled to engage in an epistemic calculus that pits that prejudice against our own epistemic agency. Chapter 2 gives an account of this epistemic calculus, this *epistemic labor*, through a series of examples. Epistemic labor exists on a continuum of clear cases, unclear cases, and borderline cases. The obvious reason for this is that testimonial injustice also exists on a continuum of cases as there are varying degrees to which credibility is deflated and varying degrees to which a negative stereotype is activated upon a marginalized speaker. The most severe cases of epistemic labor are cases where the material threat (e.g., fines and penalties, job loss, or loss of opportunity for other material goods) or bodily threat (e.g., incarceration, violence, death) to the marginalized knower makes the stakes for "knowing wrong," or failing to represent our beliefs as the *dominant* knower interprets them, dangerous. The most severe cases of epistemic labor result in a kind of *epistemic dissonance* where the marginalized knower recognizes that it is safer to misrepresent their beliefs or disavow their beliefs than to report what they know accurately. I call the latter phenomenon, *epistemic disavowal.* Unfortunately, it is easy enough to imagine such cases. Consider a case where a racist police officer stops and questions an Black or brown pedestrian about a nearby crime. The pedestrian is compelled, in some sense, to have some awareness of what the police officer *wants to know* or *will hear* in order to avoid the situation escalating to material or bodily threat. In cases like this, the consequences of "knowing wrong" can be very serious.

If epistemic injustice involves harming a knower in terms of their capacity as a knower, then severe cases of epistemic labor constitute the limit case for epistemic injustice. This is because it involves marginalized knowers consciously giving up our own epistemic selfhood. There are a variety of social phenomena that come to mind as perpetrators of, or traffickers in, this severe kind of epistemic labor. One such phenomena in the context of the U.S. justice system is plea-dealing or plea-bargaining. Here the case of Kalief Browder comes to mind. Browder's case was, for a time, the subject of much public attention. The facts are as follows:

On May 15, 2010, 16-year old Kalief Browder and his friend were stopped by police on East 186th Street in the Bronx section of New York City. They were questioned about the theft of a backpack containing a few valuables. They consented to be searched but none of the valuables were found in their possession. Browder and his friend were taken to the local precinct and processed through central booking in the Bronx County Criminal Court. Browder was charged with grand larceny, robbery, and assault. Unable to post the $3,000 bail, Browder was sent to jail on Rikers Island where he was held for almost 3 years awaiting trial. Browder spent almost 800 days in solitary confinement, engaged in at least six separate suicide attempts, and suffered consistent physical and psychological abuse by officers and fellow inmates. The charges against Browder were eventually dismissed and he was released in May 2013 after 31 court appearances. He finally got to go home. Two years later Kalief Browder committed suicide at the age of 22.

During Browder's years awaiting trial he was offered, and ultimately refused, plea deals on multiple occasions. As Browder himself said, "The judge told me if I plead guilty I will be released that same day, but I didn't do it." He added: "You're not going to make me say I did something just so I can go home. The way I looked at it if I got to stay here just to prove that I am innocent, then so be it" (Pitts, Yu, and Effron 2015). In significant part, Browder's beliefs were determined by his awareness of the epistemic environment in which he found himself. The judge, in particular, had normative expectations of what Browder ought believe about himself and his role in his own incarceration. This is perhaps why he was encouraged to take a plea deal despite declarations of his own innocence. Browder did not belong to a social group privileged enough to have his assertions of innocence meaningfully heard. Instead, he was forced to recognize his circumstances as marred by systemic bias and prejudice and to make strategic epistemic choices that reflected, as far as he could, his own epistemic agency.

What the judge, the court, and the prosecutor asked of Browder (as they do many others as well) was to assert guilt despite claims of innocence. Judges, prosecutors, and defense lawyers have an epistemic responsibility not only to convey plea information accurately but to be cognizant of how plea-bargaining fits into the wider landscape of discriminatory behaviors. Such a landscape is fertile ground for willful ignorance of the negative biases and prejudices that infect criminal cases. This is the landscape that we must take as the backdrop for Browder's case. The epistemic injustice here is best explained as the institutional pressure exerted against marginalized knowers to disavow their own epistemic agency in the face of physical and psychological threat. The non-epistemic stakes are so severe for marginalized knowers that we are often compelled to be complicit in our own self-silencing. We are compelled to knowingly surrender our ability to represent our own beliefs accurately and to *testify against our epistemic selves* (e.g., admit guilt because everyone thinks you guilty anyway).

To be clear, I am not claiming that all criminal defendants offered plea deals engage in self-silencing. Nor am I claiming that those who claim innocence are all innocent. There are clearly cases where the accused admits guilt and accepts a plea deal because they are, in fact, guilty. I also do not ignore the fact that plea deals are, for better or for worse, a part of the procedural dynamics of the criminal justice system. As Justice Anthony Kennedy writes in the majority opinion in *Missouri v. Frye, No. 10-444*:

> The reality is that plea bargains have become so central to the administration of the criminal justice system that defense counsel have responsibilities in the plea bargain process, responsibilities that must be met to render the adequate assistance of counsel that the Sixth Amendment requires in the criminal process at critical stages. Because ours "is for the most part a system of pleas, not a system of trials," it is insufficient simply to point to the guarantee of a fair trial as a backstop that inoculates any errors in the pretrial process (U.S. *No. 10-444*, 2012).[1]

Real testimonial justice ought to require that dominant knowers intervene in the social institutions that allow testimonial injustice to prevail. As Justice Kennedy implies in the above quotation, we cannot simply point to the fact that our social institutions are just if the administration of those institutions is unjust. I come back to this point in chapter 5. For marginalized knowers in hostile epistemic environments, where communicating what one knows is a fraught process, the price of ignoring the material or bodily stakes of saying *what one knows as one knows it*, can be unimaginably high. In Browder's case, the price that he paid was his life.

Chapter 3 takes up the twin issues of dominant knowing and willful ignorance. In the first part of the chapter, I consider Miranda Fricker's argument for hermeneutical injustice rooted in hermeneutical marginalization. This argument rests on the idea that, due to structural identity prejudice, marginalized knowers often do not participate in the shared meaning-making of collective hermeneutical resources. This lack of participation means that critical social concepts may not be included in the collective repertoire resulting in situations where marginalized knowers cannot render intelligible important aspects of our social experiences. Hermeneutical marginalization leads to the subsequent hermeneutical injustice. Here I question the idea that the lack of access to shared meaning-making can make marginalized social experiences unintelligible. I argue instead that claims of unintelligibility are rooted in problems of *naming* or *christening* social experiences not in understanding or communicating those experiences. In the second part of the chapter, I offer an overview of critiques of hermeneutical injustice offered by Rebecca Mason, José Medina, Charles Mills, and Gaile Pohlhaus, Jr. My primary goal is to explore the tension between the concept of hermeneutical marginalization and Pohlhaus's concept of willful hermeneutical ignorance. Specifically, I consider the question of whether hermeneutical marginalization is really a case of dominant knowers *failing to know* or *failing to use* truly collective hermeneutical resources as they fail to consider the epistemic resources of marginalized knowers. If hermeneutical marginalization really stems from willful ignorance, then how should we conceptualize degrees of ignorance and degrees of responsibility for that ignorance? I suggest that while we may think of willful ignorance as existing along a continuum of cases between what Medina calls, "not needing to know" and "needing not to know," the social oppression and social domination that marginalized knowers face is so historically patterned and socially ubiquitous that *failing to know* is really tantamount to an active, willful "needing not to know," and is thus always epistemically irresponsible. I use Robin DiAngelo's work on white fragility to suggest that dominant knowers protect these epistemically irresponsible beliefs, and do not hold them to sufficient epistemic scrutiny, in order to preserve their own social dominance.

In chapter 4, I consider the question of how dominant knowers and marginalized knowers can engage in meaningful discussions about shared or collective meaning-making. I begin the chapter by thinking through the lens of the epistemology of disagreement and ordinary cases of epistemic disagreement. I consider what happens in the case where the disagreeing parties are epistemic equals, or epistemic peers, and then through the case where one party is an epistemic inferior and the other is an epistemic superior. I think through how disagreement is impacted by unjust credibility deficits and unjust assignments of epistemic inferiority, similar to what occurs in related cases of testimonial injustice. Here I come back to the discussion from chapter 1 about the role negative bias and prejudice—and particularly negative *implicit* bias—plays in assignments of credibility. I look to recent work on the self-regulation of implicit bias and consider the potential of self-regulation in generating less prejudicial disagreements. I consider four model type of self-regulation of implicit bias and prejudice: (1) strategy models, (2) discrepancy models, (3) IAT models, and (4) egalitarian goal models. Similar to Fricker's account of testimonial virtue, I argue that strategies for self-regulation are flawed in many overlapping ways, including that most strategies fail to be sufficiently diachronic and fail to rule out alternate explanations for the perceived modifications of belief and behavior. That is, most strategies for self-regulation are inconclusive mechanisms for less biased and prejudicial disagreements and inconclusive mechanisms for remediating persistent testimonial injustice.

If it is not possible for dominant knowers to regulate implicit bias and engage in disagreement without deflating the credibility of marginalized knowers, i.e., making unjust assignments of epistemic inferiority, then are all disagreements between power asymmetrical knowers unjust? That is, does implicit bias make *all* communicative exchanges between power asymmetrical knowers unjust? It may be the case that dominant knowers cannot "hear well" due to their epistemic privilege, i.e., the privilege to shape and reinforce the collective (dominant) epistemic resources, but they can choose to understand *how* their privilege distorts the epistemic landscape for both themselves and for marginalized knowers. Here I explore the idea of *evolving epistemic frameworks* or social spaces for knowledge-production where social power asymmetries are made explicit. In evolving epistemic frameworks, sympathetic dominant knowers temporarily renounce their epistemic privilege and/or use their privilege to amplify marginalized epistemic resources by way of selective silences or by redirecting dominant resources toward marginalized knowers. Sympathetic dominant knowers serve as *epistemic allies* by extending social power to marginalized knowers and, by extension, to marginalized epistemologies. I explore the concept of evolving epistemic frameworks in light of the 2018 case of the Parkland, Florida school shooting and the subsequent student-led movement against gun violence. In this example, the primarily white victims of gun violence in Parkland, Florida were able to amplify the speech of primarily Black and Hispanic victims of gun violence through their engagement with activist groups in Chicago and Santa Fe. In these cases, and by ceding some social and epistemic power, the Parkland activists were able to draw attention to marginalized testimonies and marginalized epistemic resources. But evolving epistemic frameworks are highly unstable solutions for epistemic justice. This is because they exist within the confines of dominant knowing and thus will almost always be plagued by issues of social power.

In chapter 5, I argue that because evolving epistemic frameworks are not grounded in the type of social and political change that restructures distributions of social power, they cannot permanently restructure *epistemic power* in a way that leads to long-lasting epistemic justice. Epistemic equality cannot be fully realized without social and political equality. This entails that much of the theorizing about epistemic justice will be, at least practically speaking, toothless without social justice. I suggest that we should not rely on individual extensions of credibility to achieve epistemic justice, or what I call *epistemic charity*, but instead, should look to structural solutions for persistent epistemic injustice. Like a non-binding contract, dominant knowers may stop performing epistemically charitable acts at their convenience. This is because charity as a good does not depend on background social conditions *themselves* being good. This leads, I argue, to very weak notions of epistemic justice. The goal is to make epistemic justice part of our social systems and social institutions such that credibility is dispersed through systems and not by way of individual practices and behaviors. Here I look to Elizabeth

Anderson's work on epistemic justice as virtue of social institutions as a way of thinking about structural solutions. I also consider arguments by Michael Doan and Nancy Arden McHugh about how to incorporate marginalized epistemic resources, and marginalized resistant practices, into the social structuring of epistemic justice. Ultimately, I conclude that, for better or worse, all concerns about epistemic justice come back around to concerns about how social dominance, and the desire to maintain social dominance, negatively impacts the pursuit of both social justice and epistemic justice.

Finally, a note on the framing of this work. Although this project aims to center marginalized knowers and marginalized perspectives, it is important to remember that knowers can be marginalized in different ways and across different, and often multiple, axes of oppression. This makes it difficult to center all marginalized knowers as the bearers of the epistemic experiences that I describe in this project. Thus I use the terms *dominant* and *marginalized* to center primarily, but not exclusively, relationships of race-based marginalization or race-based identity power. It was not an arbitrary choice to center racial marginalization in the context of this work. One of the primary issues with social power, and particularly racial power, is the role that it plays in shaping our ways of knowing. As feminist proponents of standpoints, social locations, and ecological spaces have pointed out (Code 2006; Collins 2000; Harding 1993), social power often hides behind the rhetoric of objectivity while obscuring the ways in which it both decides and influences inquiry. Nowhere is this more true than in the case of race-based identity power. Anti-Black racism and prejudice, particularly against people in the African diaspora, constitutes one of the most (if not *the* most) persistent, aggressive, and oppressive forms of race-based prejudice in the Western world. This is not to say that other types of race-based prejudice are not persistent and oppressive as well, but that anti-Black prejudice has a particular virulence that runs parallel to and extends well beyond histories of slavery, *de facto* slavery, and violent social oppression. In the case of the United States, social dominance finds no fuller instantiation than in race-based white dominance and marginalization finds no fuller instantiation than in anti-Black racism and prejudice. Thus a focus on the dichotomy of whiteness/dominance and Blackness/marginalization will take us to the very edge of discussions of social marginalization.

Centering racial marginalization also emphasizes that the lived experiences of marginalized knowers are wedded to *ways of knowing* that are constructed by dominant knowers with the social power to make and maintain the wider epistemic landscape. This kind of malignant social construction of knowledge has serious epistemic and real-world costs. As the classical pragmatists theorized, our ways of knowing are constrained by reality but that does not mean that our ways of knowing cannot go wildly wrong. Centering racial marginalization is a project in the same epistemological tradition of looking to the social margins, e.g., marginalized standpoints and social locations, to gain a better grasp of objectivity and a better grasp of what the world *really* looks like. (Although, as I will argue in chapter 5, standpoints are not themselves unproblematic.) As Collins argues with the concept of "outsider within," considering intersections of racial identity as social locations, e.g., African-American woman, allows those with this status to theorize the most pernicious social hierarchies by using our relationship to—and from—axes of social power as an epistemic tool. Starting from this presumption, we can see that centering race is not merely a way of *speaking about* the role of race in our epistemic activities as it is a way of *speaking to* certain kinds of racialized social and epistemic experiences.

Another important aspect of centering racial marginalization rests on what most philosophers would believe to be a methodological taboo—that is, emphasizing that the *who* that is theorizing is speaking from a place of "outsider within" knowledge. Here I aim to work from my own experiences and to consciously avoid speaking for and over the experiences of marginalized others. This does not mean that I will avoid using examples or case studies of other forms of social marginalization in this project or that I can speak for all racially marginalized knowers. Following the call of Patricia Hill Collins, I use the first-person possessive pronoun, *our,* as opposed to third-person, *their,* to make the process of centering explicit, while acknowledging that not all racially marginalized knowers experience epistemic injustice in the same manner (2000, 19). There are many contexts and nuances pertaining to racial marginalization that I do not explore in this project (such as colorism, diasporic histories, linguistic diversity, internalized racism, etc.) and there are many instances where I will purposefully blur these nuances to make a broader point. I also use the terminology, *dominant knower/dominant knowing,* as shorthand for *white knower/white knowing* in most cases. When this fails to be the case, for example, in cases where the terms dominant knower/dominant knowing can be read sensibly and ambiguously in terms of other relations of identity power, I see no reason why whiteness ought to be the default as opposed to *Western, masculine, cisgender, heterosexual, abled,* and so on.

I want to stress that centering racial marginalization is complicated project. It starts from the inside-out, from me as the theorizer, to less than comfortable generalizations about types of racialized social and epistemic experiences. There are patterns of behaviors and social experiences that I will undoubtedly get wrong (or misread) and generalizations that I will make that are sure to offend. My hope is that this project is not taken as a wholesale accounting of a "centered" take on epistemic injustice but as an attempt to take seriously the proposition of centering inquiry from the margins with the goal of greater objectivity. Although this is surely problematic, as I argue in chapter 5, it is still a start. There is a larger tradition of speaking from the margins that I also invoke here. When Sojourner Truth said: "I am a woman's rights" at the Women's Rights Convention in 1851, she centered herself in the struggle for women's right to suffrage and expanded the framework for thinking about women and women's rights to include Black women and Black women's suffrage as well. Centering her race along with her gender, or the intersectional experience of racism and sexism (or a sexism that *includes* racialized bodies), was a personal act that did not, and could not, include the experiences of all Black women. But that was hardly the point. The point was to add to the discussion and to put another, often omitted, view on the table. Kristie Dotson notes that when we move our lens to focus on one element of analysis, it means leaving other elements out of the frame. Thus every analysis is, in its own way, limited to what one chooses to focus on. This does not mean that we ought to shoulder shrug, "everything has limits," and avoid finding, pushing, and challenging those limits, or to consider any analysis, particularly by women of color in philosophy, as the "sum total" of all analyses by women of color (Dotson 2014a, 4). We can and should always ask, "What has not been revealed by this particular framing?" (Dotson 2014a, 4). For myself, and for this project, I take Dotson's words to be a serious reminder that, despite our best efforts, there is always more to be done.

NOTE

1. In recent years, many books, articles, and investigative pieces have sought to illustrate the deep systemic issues with racial, ethnic, and gender identity discrimination in the U.S. criminal justice system. Here I think of works like Michelle Alexander's (2010) *The New Jim Crow: Mass Incarceration in the Age of Colorblindness;* Mogul et al.'s (2012) *Queer (In)Justice: The Criminalization of LGBT People In the United States;* Bryan Stevenson's (2014) *Just Mercy: A Story of Justice and Redemption*; and Ta-Nehisi Coates's (2015) *Between the World and Me* as critical analyses and explorations of the failure(s) of justice in the U.S. criminal justice system. To compound these analyses, the during the 2012 legislative session the Supreme Court of the United States ruled on two cases, *Missouri v. Frye, No. 10-444* and *Lafler v. Cooper, No. 10-209* expanding the rights of criminal defendants in plea bargaining. This is an explicit acknowledgement (aside from former Justice Scalia's dissenting opinion) on the part of the Supreme Court of the role that lawyer incompetence with regard to plea bargaining plays in the meting out of justice for the criminally accused. This decision was recently reaffirmed by the Supreme Court in the 2017 case, *Lee v. United States, No. 16-327.*

Chapter 1

On Testimonial Virtue and Testimonial Justice

In cases of testimony, we think of a speaker as engaging in a communicative act that implicitly or explicitly asks a hearer to entertain an assertion as true. Testimony often begins with the idea that a hearer will either accept or reject a speaker's assertion based on either the assertion itself or based on another method of justification like perception, memory, or inference. If a colleague asserts that she is catching the nine o'clock train to Philadelphia on Monday morning, we may take her assertion as true because we have no good reason to reject it, or we may take the her assertion as true because we see that she is holding a copy of a recent train schedule. But what about cases of testimonial injustice where her testimony is rejected due to a negative identity prejudice that we hold about "people like her"? For instance, what if we believe that she is mistaken because she is a woman, and we believe that women are not credible testifiers, or are not credible in relation to issues of transportation? To take this in another direction, what if our colleague is holding a train schedule that she memorized in *anticipation* of our disbelief? How should her actions, her operating on the presumption of disbelief, figure into an account of testimonial injustice? In the introduction to this book, we looked at a case of a transgender student whose complaint about the maintenance of a gender neutral restroom was met with disbelief by a buildings and grounds worker at their local college. In that case, the student softened their tone and behaved in a passive manner in order to gain epistemic uptake with the worker. How are these cases similar? How do cases like these map on to the predominant account of testimonial injustice offered by Miranda Fricker (2007)?

As mentioned in the Introduction, what is missing from the predominant account of epistemic injustice is an analysis of the myriad ways in which marginalized knowers adjust their own epistemic behaviors in the face of epistemic injustice. If my colleague holds a train schedule in anticipation of not being believed or a student softens their tone to gain a better hearing, then there are clearly methods that socially marginalized knowers use to improve unjust (or presumably unjust) testimonial outcomes. If that is the case, then one critical part of thinking through epistemic injustice, and testimonial injustice in particular, is thinking through both this type of epistemic labor on behalf of marginalized knowers and *rethinking* how dominant knowers should go about remediating this injustice. In light of this rethinking, this chapter has two distinct aims. First, I aim to rethink one of Fricker's core examples of testimonial injustice, the trial of Tom Robinson from Harper Lee's *To Kill a Mockingbird*, and what she takes to be the wrong or harm of testimonial injustice. Second, I aim to rethink how Fricker conceives of testimonial virtue as a corrective for the wrong. In my view, testimonial virtue can only serve as a partial solution for testimonial injustice because Fricker's account of testimonial injustice is incomplete without an account of epistemic labor. To illustrate this, I reason backwards to outline what testimonial virtue aims to achieve in order to see where it fails to account for this additional labor.

In the second part of this chapter, I claim that even *without* reimagining testimonial injustice in light of epistemic labor, testimonial virtue will still prove to be a problematic solution for testimonial injustice. This is because it may not be possible for dominant hearers to employ epistemically virtuous practices consistently over time; testimonial virtue may not be sufficiently diachronic. Here I consider recent research in social psychology on stereotype formation and stereotype deployment as critical cognitive roadblocks to consistently employing testimonial virtues. We are, it seems, too quick to nonconsciously divide up the world into "friend" and "foe" (or "Us" and "Them") such that it may not be possible for dominant hearers to consciously and consistently override these nonconscious dispositions in the pursuit of testimonial virtue. The goal of this section is not to suggest that Fricker's view of testimonial virtue cannot be successful in some circumstances. It is intended to emphasize the point that there are practical or operational problems inherent to *consistently* employing virtue as a mechanism for resolving persistent ethical and epistemic problems.

Fricker's analysis of testimonial injustice begins with an analysis of social power. This is described as the socially situated "capacity we have as social agents to influence how things go in the social world" (Fricker 2007, 9). Fricker divides social power into an active and passive forms. Active social power, based on the Foucauldian account of power, ties power to its active exercise ("Power exists only when it is put into action") (2007, 10). Passive social power, on the other hand, regulates the actions of others both when it is used, or active, and when the threat of its use persists. That is, passive power has the rather insidious ability to regulate our actions even when there is an absence of a subject to execute that power. In the complete absence of a subject of power, power primarily manifests in structural ways as *structural power*. This is distinct from *agential power* or the power an individual has over the actions and/or potential actions of another individual. Agential power is dependent on social context and a shared structural mechanism, i.e., a social or political institution that underwrites the agent's claim to social authority. Agential power has a face and a name while structural power does not. Social power also begets a kind of identity power. Identity power is also socially situated but is socially situated in virtue of our collective social imagination or collective construction of dominant (and conversely, marginalized) social identities. Because identity power is rooted in the collective social imagination, identity power draws its influence from the same co-extending spheres as social power.

For Fricker, identity power lies at the center of unjust testimonial exchanges. Identity power is central to the mechanism of testimony because all knowers use social stereotypes, often nonconsciously as quick and easy markers of social and epistemic credibility. As Tamar Szabó Gendler argues, social stereotypes have heuristic value and our failure to encode them, even the negative, pernicious ones, can have serious epistemic costs (2011, 37). Fricker argues that stereotypes only become epistemically and ethically problematic when the stereotype involves a negative identity prejudice. If a negative identity-prejudicial stereotype leads a dominant hearer to deflate or depress the credibility of a marginalized speaker, then the use of that identity-prejudicial stereotype has caused a case of testimonial injustice. This is a case of a social stereotype "gone wrong." However, deflating a marginalized speaker's credibility due to negative identity prejudice does not alone make a hearer culpable. There are incidental and/or circumstantial cases of testimonial injustice as well. For instance, in an incidental case of testimonial injustice a dominant hearer might deflate the credibility of marginalized speaker but that deflation might *not* be the result of an identity prejudice that tracks on to persistent, systematic injustice, e.g., an identity prejudice against vegans. To get a better sense of what is involved in a persistent and systematic cases of testimonial injustice, let's consider Fricker's central case of testimonial injustice, Tom Robinson's trial from Harper Lee's *To Kill a Mockingbird*.

Tom Robinson is a Black man in 1930s rural Alabama accused of beating and raping a young white woman named Mayella Ewell. Robinson is innocent; Mayella Ewell's beating came at the hands of her father, Bob Ewell, after she attempted to kiss Robinson. But the racial hysteria of the town and with the trial makes Robinson's innocence an empty focal point. As Fricker notes, telling the truth as he knows it is a difficult prospect for Robinson because the truth will not be what the all-white jury hears. Instead, Robinson's testimony must lie at the intersection of what is true and what the jury is *willing* to hear. Fricker argues that if Robinson does indeed report what happened between him and Ewell—highlighting her instigation and her attempt to kiss him—then he will be viewed as an impudent and "not knowing his place." However, if he fails to tell the truth then he will absolutely guarantee a guilty verdict. There is no way for Robinson's testimony to be heard without identity prejudice infecting either scenario. Despite his attempt to tell the truth, and despite the fact that both members of the Ewell family were obviously lying, Robinson is easily convicted.

Fricker describes this case as an extreme example of testimonial injustice because it is both *systematic* and *persistent*. It is systematic because it is produced by the kind of negative identity prejudices that track marginalized knowers along a variety of intersecting injustices and through multiple axes of our social lives, including education, work, housing, law, and are reinforced by social and institutional structures as well as the dominant culture. It is persistent because systematic injustices not only frame and dictate Robinson's social experiences but do so in large part because of how racial prejudice is built into the historical collective imagination. Fricker distinguishes systematic and persistent testimonial injustice from incidental or circumstantial testimonial injustice in that incidental or circumstantial injustices are not as socially or epistemically disadvantageous. Although incidental cases of testimonial injustice may still hurt the speaker, Fricker insists that it is the connection to the depth and scope of corresponding structural injustices that makes severe cases of testimonial injustice so problematic.

For Fricker, testimonial injustice and the wrong or harm of testimonial injustice exists along a gradient. The nature of these harms is twofold and rather nuanced. At first look, testimonial injustice is a "purely epistemic harm" that stems from the hearer's prejudices as it blocks the transmission of knowledge to the hearer and to the public domain (Fricker 2007, 43). The harm is that testimonial injustice gets in the way of the truth-directedness of our testimonial practices as it is "an obstacle to truth" (Fricker 2007, 43). But there is also an *ethical harm* involved in testimonial injustice. Fricker argues that the ethical harm is of greater concern because of the harm that the hearer does to the speaker. The hearer commits an intrinsic injustice, wronging the knower in their capacity as a knower. This wrong undermines a capacity that is essential to human worth, the capacity to offer knowledge to others, or, as Fricker emphasizes, *the very capacity to reason* (2007, 44). "When someone suffers a testimonial injustice," she writes, "they are degraded *qua* knower, and they are symbolically degraded *qua* human" (Fricker 2007, 44).

A speaker subjected to testimonial injustice as both a singular event or as a background condition of their social life may be subject to a wide range of practical consequences as well, e.g., a lack of professional opportunities, poor working conditions, etc. These are described as the secondary harms of testimonial injustice that stem from the primary intrinsic harm. In these cases, speakers may lose confidence in their own beliefs and/or their own intellectual abilities such that they are hindered in other social pursuits. Marginalized knowers may also lose confidence such that they stop satisfying the conditions for knowledge entirely. Consider a marginalized knower whose experience with systematic and persistent testimonial injustice is so severe that leads them to doubt that they can even perceive events correctly or report events accurately to others. Fricker's example of Marge Sherwood from Anthony Minghella's screenplay, *The Talented Mr. Ripley*, offers an example of this sort. In the screenplay, Marge's suspicions of foul play are dismissed after her boyfriend, Dickie Greenleaf, goes missing during their Italian holiday. Marge is suspicious of Dickie's new friend, Tom Ripley, after Ripley enters their life in Italy on peculiar grounds and ingratiates himself to Dickie. Her suspicions are dismissed by Dickie's father, Herbert Greenleaf, as irrational or hysterical "female intuition," causing Marge to doubt herself and her perception of Ripley's strange behaviors.

Fricker concludes that the true harm of testimonial injustice is that it excludes the speaker from trustful social dialogue and positions them within the socio-epistemic world as objects. Following Bernard Williams, she argues that engaging in trustful social dialogue helps knowers to form critical aspects of their social identity. Being excluded from these activities through systematic and persistent testimonial injustice can hinder the development of self. Echoing a line of social psychological research, Fricker claims that persistent testimonial injustice may even cause a knower to construct their social identity in terms of the negative identity-prejudicial stereotypes at the root of testimonial injustice (2007, 55–56). The idea of exclusion plays a key part in understanding why the wrong of testimonial injustice also constitutes a kind of *epistemic objectification*. Using the work of Bernard Williams and Edward Craig, Fricker suggests that, in the state of nature, the need for survival begets the need for a shared pool of knowledge and information as well as for relations of trust (2007, 109–111). If the subject of testimonial injustice is denied access to this basic epistemic relationship, then they are treated as a *source of information,* or an object of knowledge, as opposed to an *informant,* or a subject of knowledge: "He is thus demoted from subject to object, relegated from the role of active epistemic agent, and confined to the role of passive state of affairs from which knowledge might be gleaned" (Fricker 2007, 132).

If we return to the above case of Tom Robinson's trial in *To Kill a Mockingbird*, we might ask what was required in order to prevent the type of epistemic objectification that happened to him? What was required in order to make the move back from *object to subject*? What epistemic remediation measures can dominant knowers employ? Recall, however, that the type of testimonial injustice that we are concerned about does not stem from the one-off mistakes in assigning deflated credence to marginalized speakers.

We are concerned with systematic and persistent testimonial injustice that tracks onto wider structural patterns of social injustice. Thus any epistemic solution will have to account for how the operations and imaginations of structural power give license to dominant hearers to use that power in deflating marginalized testimony as well as how that power can be mitigated in order to adequately hear testimonies like Robinson's. So it is important to ask ourselves whether or not our epistemic remediation measures can address both structural *and* agential power. In Fricker's case, she argues that we ought to focus on the activities of the dominant hearer or on an *agential* solution. The goal is for the dominant hearer to develop a testimonial sensibility such that the negative perception that underwrites their prejudicial credibility judgment is positively amended and the marginalized speaker is reconceived of as a proper informant—or goes from object back to subject. The question is, how can the dominant hearer change the negative perception at the root of his credibility deflation? This question becomes particularly acute if we consider that the negative perception itself has most likely been created and maintained by larger social-structural forces and thus has been reinforced consistently and aggressively over time.

Consider how Fricker describes the epistemic failure of testimonial injustice as a failure of the dominant hearer to appropriately attend to their prejudicial habits of hearing. In the case of Tom Robinson's trial, the jury fails to attend to and correct for the ways in which their habits of hearing are infected by pervasive racist tropes and ideas. The dominant hearers' testimonial sensibilities are so tainted by identity power such that they cannot see the extent to which their *whiteness* and Robinson's *Blackness* impacts their ability to perceive him accurately. The sensibility that they lack is similar to what Lorraine Code refers to as "epistemic responsibility." Code's conception of epistemic responsibility involves being able to give a narrative account of what makes a particular knower likely to accept or reject a given *p*. Knowers need to account for (and to be responsible for) the social context of their knowing such that if a tainted line of reasoning leads to the acceptance of *p*, then the knower is responsible for narratively unpacking that poor reasoning and revising their beliefs. For Fricker, the testimonial responsibility that she asks dominant hearers to develop involves "a distinctly reflexive critical social awareness" of identity power relations that exist between speaker and hearer such that spontaneous deflations can be mitigated by a deeper reflective ability (2007, 91). The hearer must acknowledge both the loaded social context that sits behind an unjust testimonial exchange and how that context gives shape to the negative perceptions of the speaker that underwrite poor credibility judgments, and then they must amend their judgments accordingly.

Once this testimonial failure is recognized, a dominant hearer can employ testimonial virtue as an anti-prejudicial corrective mechanism. This process relies on the dominant hearer sensing, or anticipating, a negative identity-prejudicial perception or response, and moving from a spontaneous reaction to a more critical disposition. The hearer can either neutralize the prejudice by suspending their credibility judgement until more evidence is available or they can aim to inflate the speaker's credibility to make up for the initial (or anticipated) deflation. The goal is to habituate this process— this flipping of the cognitive switch—until the response becomes at least as spontaneous, or as cognitively available, as the perceptions that guided the negative credibility judgment in the first place. Fricker acknowledges that the nature of prejudice is dynamic. It may not be possible to habituate virtue with a background of constantly changing social contexts in a manner that makes virtue reflexive across all cases and scenarios. The partial attainment of testimonial virtue will be the next best thing: "Perhaps some combination of spontaneity and reflectiveness may be the ideal . . . What matters is that somehow or other one succeeds, reliably enough (through time and across a suitable span of prejudices), in correcting for prejudice in one's credibility judgements" (Fricker 2007, 98).

Notice, however, that the application of testimonial virtue only works if the relevant testimonial sensibility exists as a precondition. A dominant hearer must analyze their own stereotypes and weed out the negatively prejudicial ones. They must also be on alert for the ways in which identity power in general may infect their day-to-day perceptions of marginalized speakers. Fricker argues that in order for dominant knowers to see marginalized speakers "in epistemic colour" their perceptions need to be reencoded with a new set of heuristics, one that minimizes the near-spontaneous workings of negative identity-prejudicial stereotypes in favor of a richer "socially situated 'theory' of the competences and motivations of this or that social type in this or that context" (2007, 71). Such competences and motivations ought to be informed by the probability that the "social type" in question would be likely to tell the truth/not tell the truth in the given circumstances. The dominant hearer must also factor into this context the likelihood that the marginalized speaker's perception of the dominant hearer may be affecting the marginalized speaker's sincerity. Note that this is as close as Fricker comes to addressing the issue of how marginalized speakers adjust our testimony in light of negative social perceptions by dominant hearers. Her explanation mirrors her analysis of the case of Tom Robinson in that it focuses on how sincere/honest/truthful a marginalized speaker can be in light of what a dominant hearer is *capable* of hearing. What this analysis misses, of course, is that marginalized speakers often adjust our testimony in light of considerations beyond degree of sincerity or truthfulness. Adjusting testimony in light of an operating negative stereotype demands weighing complex social contexts, degrees of aggression

or passivity, power asymmetricity, fears of violence and/or violent repercus-
sions, the presence of by-standers or witnesses, and so on. It is a complex
matter indeed.

In cases of culpable testimonial injustice, the hope is that dominant hearers
will develop this new sensibility such that they are capable of neutralizing
negative social perceptions and giving the speaker a just hearing. Fricker
claims, however, that there is still a category of non-culpable cases where
the dominant hearer may be unable to give a just hearing because they do not
have access to the social concepts needed to adjust their perceptions and give
the speaker due credibility. In the case of *The Talented Mr. Ripley,* Dickie
Greenleaf's father, Herbert Greenleaf, did not have access to the necessary
gender concepts that would have allowed him to consider Marge Sherwood as
a trusted or credible speaker or to question his own dismissal of Marge's testimony. Because the idea of gender prejudice was not a significant part of the
collective social imagination in the 1950s, the dismissal of Marge's testimony
was merely an example of moral and epistemic bad luck (2007, 101). We
might ask what makes Marge Sherwood's case importantly different than the
case of Tom Robinson? Surely, one could make a similar claim about racial
prejudice? Fricker claims that Robinson's case is different because in his case
the testimonial injustice occurred in the context of a jury trial. Fricker argues
that paying close attention to the available evidence is required for the jurors
due to the "heightened testimonial experience afforded by the trial" (2007,
90). However, it is still difficult to see why the context of a jury trial would
reduce as opposed to heighten the jurors' perceptions of race and race-based
prejudices. In fact, without the trial, it is hard to see what would make Tom
Robinson's case at all different from the case of Marge Sherwood.

Fricker focuses on the trial as the context by which the jurors ought to have
reflected on their negative perceptions of Tom Robinson and employed testimonial virtue as a corrective measure for how those perceptions depressed
their judgment of Tom's credibility. She argues that the jurors had "ample
opportunity to grasp and make good the conflict between the distrust which
their corrupted sensibility spontaneously delivers and the trust which a proper
attention to the evidence would inspire" (Fricker 2007, 89–90). According
to Fricker's analysis, we are to believe that the context of the trial and the
demand for justice (or, at least, the *truth*) would make the jurors more epistemically responsible. But it is not at all clear why this would be the case. The
jurors are depressing or deflating Robinson's credibility due to their perception of him (and "people like him") as being less than credible. Similar to the
case of Herbert Greenleaf, to override their negative perception of Robinson,
the jurors would have to have access to the necessary racial concepts to
recognize their own complicity in employing racial stereotypes in the first
place. Why would the jurors have better access to the necessary concepts to

see their own corrupted perception of Tom Robinson than Herbert Greenleaf would have to see his own corrupted perception of Marge Sherwood? Are we to believe that a concern for appropriate attention to evidence is enough to override racist perceptions in one case but not enough to override gendered perceptions in the other? Perhaps this *is* the case but it is not at all clear why it would be so.

It is important to remember that both of Fricker's examples invoke fictional universes—narrative constructions where what the characters do and do not know is circumscribed by authorial intent. That is, it is Harper Lee's social and epistemic worldview that shapes the story of Tom Robinson. If we are to extrapolate from fiction in the way that Fricker does by extending the fictional world into real, historical realities, then it may prove more useful to think through real historical examples with real epistemic parallels. Consider the case of the Scottsboro Boys, where nine Black teenagers were falsely accused of raping two white women, Victoria Price and Ruby Bates, on a train in Scottsboro, Alabama in 1931. This case resembles the case of Tom Robinson in many respects but is also very different in potentially instructive ways. First of all, the legal environment surrounding the case of the Scottsboro Boys involved active discussions about the racial makeup of juries and the possibility of fair jury trials for Black Americans, and particularly Black men, in the American South. F. Raymond Daniell wrote a series of articles in the *New York Times* between 1931 and 1937 about the case specifically chronicling the frustration of the defense attorney, Samuel Leibowitz, the International Labor Defense, the NAACP, and other related organizations, at the possibility of the Scottsboro Boys receiving a just hearing at trial. During the trial of one of the Scottsboro Boys, Charles Weems, Daniell captured Leibowitz's frustration at the flagrant violations of legal norms by the prosecution:

> "I'm sick and tired of this sanctimonious hypocrisy," [Leibowitz] shouted . . . [referring] to the string of farmers called by the State to bolster up the testimony of Mrs. Price as "trained seals" and "performers in a flea circus." He accused [the State] flatly of supporting evidence favorable to the defense, declaring that this was a further reason to suspect that the whole case against the Negroes was manufactured in Mrs. Price's head to save herself and her hobo companions from vagrancy arrests. The assertions of lawyers for the State that Negroes fare the same as white men in the courts of Northern Alabama was so much "poppycock," said Mr. Leibowitz, calling the formalities of the trial a mere travesty of justice. (1937)

Legal historian Michael J. Klarman argues that the decrease of lynchings in the 1930s in conjunction with the prospect of federal anti-lynching laws may have led to the use of jury trials as methods of formalized lynchings for Blacks in the South: "The Scottsboro defendants received precisely the sort of 'justice' that often prevailed in trials that substituted for lynchings. Both local newspapers treated the defendants as obviously guilty even before the trial (2009, 383). He writes:

> In such cases, guilt or innocence usually mattered little. As one white south-erner candidly remarked in 1933, "If a white woman is prepared to swear that a Negro either raped or attempted to rape her, we see to it that the Negro is executed." Prevailing racial norms did not permit white jurors to believe a black man's word over that of a white woman; prevailing gender norms did not allow defense counsel to closely interrogate a white woman about allega-tions involving sex. As one contemporary southern newspaper observed, the honor of a white woman was more important than the life of a black man. And because most southern white men believed that black males secretly lusted after "their" women, they generally found such rape allegations credible. (Klarman 2009, 382)

This is all to say that the concepts needed for some semblance of legal justice in the Scottsboro case may have existed at the time, e.g., the Civil Rights Act of 1875, *Strauder v. West Virginia* (1880), *Plessy v. Ferguson* (1896), but concepts needed in the *social imagination* of the relevant perpetrators, i.e., all-white juries, may have existed, but *may not have been cognitively accessible*, at the very same time. Overt racist attitudes, along with the per-vasiveness of Jim Crow laws in the South, made social and epistemic access to the necessary social concepts to exonerate the Scottsboro Boys (and Tom Robinson) extremely limited. When the U.S. Supreme Court decided to overturn one of the convictions in the Scottsboro case in *Norris v. Alabama* (1935) because Black people were systematically and unlawfully left off of jury rolls (thus producing *de facto* all-white juries) in violation of the Equal Protection Clause of the Fourteenth Amendment, the argument at the time of the trial was that the racial makeup of juries and the impacts of exclud-ing Black citizens from jury service could not be reasonably ignored. These legal arguments heightened the idea that "attending to the evidence" was of critical importance and that prejudicial jury construction may produce sham convictions. Outside of the South, and even as close as the mid-South, pub-lic perception was turning against the women (who had retracted their rape accusations) and toward the innocence of the Scottsboro Boys. As Klarman notes: Leading southern white journalists such as Douglas Southall Freeman of the *Richmond New Leader* and Josephus Daniels of the *Raleigh News and Observer* expressed outrage over the second round of convictions in light of the Scottsboro Boys' probable innocence. The *Chattanooga News* declared that "we cannot conceive of a civilized community taking human lives on the strength of the miserable affair" (2000, 66).

This would suggest a climate where it was at least *plausible* for white Southern jurors to perceive Black defendants as a credible testifier but I think this view is mistaken. The problem is not that most white Southerners could not conceive of a world where Black men might be innocent but they could not conceive of a world where Black men might be innocent while white women *were not*. If you note the language used by white Southerners at the time, there was a distinction being made between *criminal guilt* and *social allowance*. The Scottsboro Boys may not have been guilty of a crime but the mere idea that they were innocent, and that Victoria Price and Ruby Bates were *not innocent,* could not be socially tolerated. In such cases, you can see how "attention to evidence" would be entirely beside the point. The issue is not one of evidence but of social imagination and allowing the relevant social concepts to critically impinge upon white Southern reality. To find the Scottsboro Boys innocent would have required access to social concepts that did not sufficiently cohere with the related concepts of white supremacy and the supremacy of white women's fragility and virtue—even over Black lives. It would, for white Southerners, poke a conceptual hole in the social and political landscape that reigned in the American South. As one white Southerner told an investigator from the ACLU: "We white people just couldn't afford to let these niggers off because of the effect it would have on other niggers" (Klarman 2009, 383). I highlight this case to say that in real life, as opposed to fiction, people are constantly making the world as they go along. Social concepts are not fixed insomuch as they are invoked when they are needed. That is, they are invoked, reframed, and redrawn on a contextual basis and when other social pressures and social forces—positive or negative, moral or immoral—make it necessary or even convenient to do so. After the public outcry, one white Alabamian states that he "might have been for acquittin' [the Scottsboro Boys] at the first trial," suggesting an ability to reframe or redraw the social concept of "Black guilt," but goes on to say, "now after all this stink's been raised, we've got to hang 'em," backtracking and re-invoking a concept of social allowance (Klarman 2009, 389–390).

A similar but not quite so parallel case can be made about Herbert Greenleaf and Marge Sherwood from *The Talented Mr. Ripley*. Consider that the white, upper class background that frames the narrative has a particular social context of its own. Herbert Greenleaf is a rich shipping magnate who is, by all accounts, financing the extended Italian vacation of his son, Dickie, and his girlfriend, Marge. Unlike Tom Ripley, neither Dickie nor Marge work or seem at all concerned with money. Dickie, like his father, is a Princeton man, and we can reasonably assume that Marge is of similar pedigree, an upper class socialite, perhaps a graduate of one of the elite Seven Sisters colleges. In the screenplay, Dickie intends to marry Marge and will most likely return to New York to work in the family business. A character like Herbert Greenleaf would expect his son to marry a woman from a good family and of the same social class. As Herbert does not object to Marge, one can only assume that she satisfies this role. Marge is not considered to be a silly fling, or a woman beneath contempt, she is considered to be a suitable match for Dickie. Although Herbert Greenleaf may be unable to develop a critical consciousness about gender, it is hard to imagine that he views Marge as entirely epistemically untrustworthy. If he does deem her epistemically untrustworthy, as the 1999 screenplay suggests, then it is hard to imagine that the perception that generated this credibility judgment is in fact as non-culpable as Fricker suggests.

As an East Coast industrialist in the 1950s, the background of Herbert Greenleaf's life would be one of the white, Western, Protestant, hetero-normative post–World War II nuclear family. On the surface, the rhetoric of the day for white middle-class American women focused on women in the home, or going to college for their "M.R.S." degrees, suburbanization, and family-first social values. Such a social environment would indeed suggest a dearth of critical gender concepts accessible to Herbert Greenleaf. However, history has also shown this period as one reifying an informal caste system for American women. Lower-income, and mostly minority women, remained in the workforce by necessity, cleaning homes and taking care of the children of white families. While some of these women went to college, or secretarial school, or took on careers outside of homes as teachers, secretaries, and social workers, their wealthier white counterparts lived as non-working housewives, socialites, expatriates, artists and hobbyists. This class-based and race-based categorization of women would have sat in the background of Greenleaf's experiences. It is the system by which Marge Sherwood is determined to be an acceptable match for Dickie Greenleaf. Although Herbert Greenleaf may have failed to perceive *all* women as credible, it seems improbable that Marge Sherwood would have failed to be included in the category of credible, epistemically trustworthy women.

It is worth noting that when we jump from Anthony Minghella's 1999 adapted screenplay of *The Talented Mr. Ripley* to Patricia Highsmith's 1955 novel of the same name, Marge Sherwood is written with far more epistemic authority and her dealings with Herbert Greenleaf take on a rather different tenor. Marge calls Herbert Greenleaf to discuss finding Dickie's treasured rings among Ripley's personal items, entertaining the possibility that Dickie may have killed himself. Marge shares this news with Ripley (to his pleasure) and notes that Herbert Greenleaf agreed with her assessment. When Herbert Greenleaf arrived with Detective McCarron to question Ripley about

Dickie's disappearance and probable suicide, Marge was not asked to excuse herself in the discussion of the events, instead, her views on Dickie's disappearance were taken as reasonably credible by both the detective and by Dickie's father. In Highsmith's novel, it is Marge and Ripley who are mostly in discussion with the detective with Herbert Greenleaf sitting slumped off in the corner. Marge's responses are sometimes challenged by the detective but she is still treated as a reliable witness and afforded a substantial degree of credibility. This seems right for both the social circumstances of the novel and for Marge's social place within the context of those circumstances. The point is—as small as it might seem—Highsmith assigned Marge Sherwood greater credibility in her 1955 novel that she subsequently had in Minghella's 1999 retelling of the novel.

Using fictional examples to explore the shape and dimension of race-based and gender-based epistemic injustice can be a fraught endeavor. The critical epistemic points are found in the details of the real circumstances that give fiction its shape, not in the fiction itself. This is because fiction can render the background conditions of its characters' lives more inert than they are or would be in real life. They can also render the characters themselves more inert than they would be in real life. Like Harriet Beecher Stowe's Uncle Tom from *Uncle Tom's Cabin,* Tom Robinson's character serves more as a placeholder for the white imagination of a passive Black victim than as a complex character representative of the lived experiences of Southern Black men in the grips of white supremacy. Although these may appear to be tangential gripes about Fricker's main examples, I think that the use of fictional characters and fictional situations only obscures more complex social and epistemic realities. I would argue, although I will not do so here, that if we look instead to only real life cases, there are probably no true instances of non-culpable testimonial injustice as characterized by the Greenleaf example. That is, there are no cases where the needed social concepts are entirely unavailable, or underdeveloped, in the collective social imagination such that the resulting testimonial injustice would fail to be epistemically and morally blameworthy. Instead, I would make a distinction between what an individual is in a *position to know* and what an individual is in a *position to hear*. This is because our social concepts, and the making and revising of them at the structural level, are probably more dynamic than our individual ability to accept and employ them.

If we return to Fricker's argument for a moment, and the claim that testimonial justice is the act of recognizing and neutralizing negative prejudice, we might argue now that even if the relevant concepts are there, the jury may still fail to adopt them. In the case of Tom Robinson, this view suggests that Robinson will find testimonial justice if and when the jurors see how their negative identity prejudices impact their perception of his credibility and adjust their credences accordingly. But even in the case where this does occur, is this all that there is to testimonial justice? What happens to this view of testimonial justice if we consider the case from Robinson's perspective? To note, and in a very real sense, I recognize that such credibility adjustments can be of critical importance. If the jurors employed testimonial virtue, then perhaps Robinson would not have been convicted and subsequently killed while trying to escape prison. If we are to be brute utilitarians for a moment, applying testimonial virtue could have led to a better outcome. However, if we take another perspective, perhaps a more Kantian one, it may be the case that the jury recognizes its own prejudice, adjusts their assessment of Robinson's credibility, and still fails to see his inherent humanity. Acknowledging and fixing an unjust prejudice is a fine goal but it is a goal that can be achieved while remaining entirely self-directed and self-interested. It is possible to want to be a better, less prejudicial person, and to have a positive impact on the lives of others, while still failing to see other people *as people*.

Fricker's account of testimonial justice appears too unidirectional. While there are clear benefits for marginalized speakers, it says nothing of the wrong or harm *as experienced* by those who are marginalized. Fricker claims that the harm of testimonial injustice is in making marginalized speakers *objects*, or in undermining, or taking away our humanity, but this characterization, however well-intended, is insulting. Dominant hearers may deny the humanity of marginalized speakers by way of identity prejudice but that does not mean that marginalized speakers see ourselves this way. Being seen as less credible does not *make* one less credible unless one wants to argue that the dominant framework used for judging credibility is the *only* framework worth using. What it *really* means is that the dominant framework dictating who bears the perceptual markers of credibility is epistemically corrupt. Marginalized speakers work very hard to make ourselves heard within corrupted frameworks and with varying degrees of success. (I come back to this argument in chapter 2.) Thus it is only a partial achievement of testimonial justice to dole out a bit more credibility within a corrupted framework on marginalized speakers' behalf.

Consider that Tom Robinson was still compelled to compensate for a social and epistemic framework that assumed he was untrustworthy because of the color of his skin. Even in the scenario where testimonial injustice does not occur (say, in the highly improbable case where he was exonerated by the jury), Robinson would still have expected this epistemic environment to be polluted by racial prejudice. He would have still felt forced to be careful with the truth, to engage in self-denigrating niceties, and to present himself as passively as possible to avoid bodily or material harm at the hands of the jury. How exactly does Fricker's account of testimonial justice account for this epistemic and psychic harm? What is interesting about Fricker's account is that she is not unaware of Tom's epistemic labor. She notices the lengths that Tom must go through to approximate the truth without telling it entirely. She notices how he must anticipate the racist reaction to his testimony and must work within those constraints. The harm he faces, as we quickly learn as readers, is not just an epistemic harm. It is not merely that his ability to assert the truth and/or represent his beliefs by his own lights is impeded by prejudice. It is that he is forced to inhibit himself, to police his own beliefs, in order to avoid the harm of imprisonment or possible death.

Here I think we can begin to see one of the main issues with testimonial virtue as the mechanism for remediating testimonial injustice. It falls short in terms of thinking about justice from the perspective of those who are harmed by unjust acts. As Thoreau famously said, it takes two to speak the truth—a speaker and a hearer—but both need to be freed from the ways in which negative prejudice and bias infect the transmission of truth in order to do so. The dominant hearer needs to acknowledge and correct for negative prejudice, yes, but the marginalized speaker needs to be free from the *expectation* of that prejudice as well. That expectation is the toxic residue of socially and epistemically polluted environments; environments that can be polluted in two primary ways, externally, by social and cultural forces and, internally, by the ways that mind comes to perceive and arrange the social world. In the second part of this chapter, I consider this issue with testimonial virtue as a remedy for testimonial injustice. Leaving aside the unidirectional nature of testimonial virtue, the practice of testimonial virtue itself may still fail to achieve its goal because the exercise of virtue is subject to multiple cognitive roadblocks. Dominant hearers are likely to find themselves in situations where they cannot express testimonial virtue because they have been primed for too long to see the world as one of "Us" and "Them," and negative stereotypes are too cognitively *sticky,* and testimonial injustice too pervasive, for the consistent application of virtue over time.

We do not call a person "good" because they perform one good action. We call a person "good" because they perform in ways that are considered good consistently and over time. This does not mean that they do not make mistakes along the way, or that they do not perform any misdeeds, it means that, on the whole, their actions and behaviors are what we would call good. Epistemic virtue ought to work in a similar fashion. We ought not call a hearer epistemically virtuous for one-off acts of epistemic virtue. Instead, we ought to call a hearer epistemically virtuous for being able to perform virtue in a sufficiently diachronic manner. If there are serious roadblocks to a dominant hearer being able to perform virtue in this manner, then we ought to rethink the moral and epistemic value of theories of virtue. One important roadblock that I consider below is how negative identity-prejudicial stereotypes, in their formation and maintenance, may be more difficult to *unlearn* than we think because we might be cognitively predisposed to the enhanced learning of them. If this is the case, then this may also make prejudicial perceptions generated from negative stereotypes much more difficult to consciously correct through the exercise of epistemic virtue. Consider the value of stereotypes as a heuristic in general. Fricker argues that stereotypes can operate in good, bad, and neutral ways. In their best form, stereotypes can help us to make easy generalizations about a speaker's epistemic trustworthiness. Citing recent work in social psychology, Fricker claims that knowers would not be able to make credibility judgments in the fashion that we need to—quickly and reflexively—without the aid of stereotypes. Epistemic issues only arise when the social generalizations made between a social group and an attribute are generated due to a negative identity prejudice. This is because negative identity prejudices are judgments formed and maintained with a blatant disregard for proper evidence. For this reason, they are epistemically culpable.

However, there are cases where we learn or encode stereotypes *because* of a cognitive disposition toward correlating negative attributes or behaviors patterns with socially marginalized groups. In these cases, our learning of stereotypes skews decidedly negative. Recent research in experimental psychology conducted by a research group at University College London and led by the cognitive neuroscientist, Hugo Spiers, investigated this peculiar correlation. Extending the research of David Hamilton and Robert Gifford on illusory correlations, Spiers et al. sought to isolate the regions of the brain that are used in the formation of prejudicial attitudes. The UCL research group hypothesized that the results of the fMRI would mirror Hamilton and Gifford's original conclusion that groups tend to form illusory correlations between negative or undesirable behaviors and minority groups due to the over-attribution of undesirable traits to minority groups. In the original study, Hamilton and Gifford gave research participants positive or desirable behaviors and negative or undesirable behaviors about two social groups, Group A and Group B. Group A was larger than Group B and desirable traits were assigned with the same frequency to each group. Still, the study revealed that participants consistently overattributed undesirable, or negative behavior traits, to the minority group despite the fact that the percentage of behaviors were identical between the two social groups.

Spiers et al. reproduced the study with fMRI and found that not only did the study participants overattribute negative traits to the minority social group, but that they had more extensive learning of the negative minority group traits than the positive minority group traits, suggesting that the brain may be predisposed to learning or encoding negative minority traits over positive ones:

These findings provide new insights into the brain regions involved in the formation of prejudice and support the view that the anterior temporal lobe plays a prominent role in learning and representing social–emotional conceptual knowledge . . . Although we had predicted that our participants would show slower learning of the valence of the minority groups, mirroring past work on the "illusory correlation" effect (Hamilton & Gifford, 1976; Murphy et al., 2011), we did not predict that learning would be more extensive over the learning blocks for the negative groups than the positive groups . . . Furthermore, evidence suggests that negative behaviors are judged as more diagnostic of a person's true character than positive behaviors (Cone & Ferguson, 2015), which would privilege negative behaviors for learning (Spiers et al. 2016, 12).

Although far from conclusive, the findings of Spiers et al. complicates the argument that stereotypes can be fundamentally neutral as they pertain to learning and employing social generalizations. For whatever reason, *in actu*, the activity of the anterior temporal lobe suggests that the brain, when learning, is predisposed to more extensive learning of negative traits of minority groups as well as predisposed to considering such traits as representative of that minority social group. Spiers et al. note, "[the] finding that activity in the anterior temporal lobe tracks changes in the perceived valence of the different social groups provides, [is] to our knowledge, the first evidence that this region is involved in the acquisition of prejudicial intergroup attitudes" (2006, 11). This evidence suggests that the social generalizations or stereotypes that underwrite our spontaneous credibility judgments may often be negatively prejudicial at their source, at least as they pertain to minority social groups. Although the findings of Spiers et al. do not point to the impossibility of consciously neutralizing spontaneous negative stereotypes, they do point to a problem with *habituating* that practice. This is because the study points to a cognitive disposition that may make such negative stereotypes *stickier*, or more difficult to unlearn, than Fricker's account of testimonial virtue imagines. Consistent applications of testimonial virtue will have to battle against the nonconscious cognitive mechanisms that help to generate our worst perceptive and evaluative selves.

A further complication arises when look to a different category of research from social psychology and neurobiology. Carsten De Dreu et al. from Leiden University and the University of Amsterdam conducted a series of experiments using an Implicit Association Test, or IAT, along with Phillipa Foot's thought experiment, the Trolley Problem, on a group of Dutch males. The subjects were given 24 IUs of oxytocin (or a placebo) in order to study the effects of the neurohypophysial hormone on intergroup attitudes. The researchers used typical in-group targets for the experiment, Dutch males, along with socially significant out-group targets for the region, Middle Eastern immigrants and

Germans citizens. The study found that the Dutch males who were administered the 24 IUs of oxytocin were more likely to exhibit in-group favoritism toward their fellow Dutch males as well as increased out-group bias toward both Middle Eastern immigrants and German citizens. The study also found that the Dutch males who were administered oxytocin were also more likely to show in-group favoritism on the IAT and were more likely to divert the trolley car in the Trolley Problem thought experiment toward those with Middle Eastern and/or German names. That is, in the traditional trolley scenario where by-standers are asked whether or not they would re-route an out-of-control trolley car toward one person instead of five people, the Dutch male participants were less likely to re-route the trolley car if one of the five had a Middle Eastern or German name (Sapolsky 2017, 116–117). For reference's sake, it is important to remember that up to 60–70 percent of all respondents to the Trolley Problem think that the car *should be* re-routed or diverted away from the five toward the one person. In general, the researchers found that the Dutch participants were simply more likely to exhibit *explicit* out-group derogation and intergroup bias in these cases. They describe their conclusion as follows:

> Through its influence on in-group favoritism, oxytocin contributes to the development of intergroup bias and preferential treatment of in-group over out-group members. Because such unfair treatment triggers negative emotions, violent protest, and aggression among disfavored and excluded individuals (49), by stimulating in-group favoritism, brain oxytocin may trigger a chain reaction toward intense between-group conflict. This possibility questions the rather widespread view of oxytocin as a "cuddle chemical" or "love drug" (24). There is no doubt that oxytocin is implicated in the development of trust (10, 18), empathy, and prosociality (11), but these tendencies appear limited to individuals belonging to one's in-group (16, 17). Thus, rather than making humans prosocial, oxytocin functions to strengthen an evolutionary evolved and rather functional tendency to discriminate between in-group and out-group as well as to give members of one's own group preferential treatment. Such ethnocentrism has adaptive value to individuals and their groups but, unfortunately, also paves the way for intergroup bias, conflict, and violence. (De Dreu et al. 2011, 1265)

What we can take away from the findings of De Dreu et al. is that our reaction to oxytocin makes our brains deeply protective of ourselves and those we consider to be *like us* and deeply wary, and sometimes outright hostile, toward those we consider different from us. It enhances our perception of the world as divided into "Us" and "Them." As neuroendocrinologist Robert Sapolsky writes of De Dreu's studies on oxytocin: "[Oxytocin] makes us more prosocial to Us and worse to everyone else. That's not generic prosociality. That's ethnocentrism and xenophobia. In other words, the actions of these neuropeptides depend dramatically on context" (2017, 117). In the context of a testimonial exchange involving a marginalized speaker and a dominant hearer, these factors may render moot even the most sympathetic dominant hearer's epistemically virtuous intentions simply due to an overprotective neurochemical reaction. A dominant hearer who aims to practice testimonial virtue will have to contend with more than just the negative identity prejudices that underwrite their credibility judgments, depending on the context, they may find themselves at war with their own neurochemistry as well.

My aim is not to overstate the problems with testimonial virtue on the grounds a few studies or to suggest that they make the practice of testimonial virtue impossible. I only aim to point out that there are myriad ways in which negative stereotyping, biases, and prejudice run deep in terms of our ability to "turn them off" voluntarily or at will. I come back to this issue in chapter 4. Understanding the process of negative stereotyping, for example, requires us to examine stereotypes at two levels of analysis: 1) how we are socialized into the *types* of negative stereotypes that influence our spontaneous credibility assessments, and 2) how the *process* of negative stereotyping arranges the boundaries of our social world via specific cognitive and neurochemical mechanisms. This is further complicated by the manner in which we form negative stereotypes about minority social groups and the speed in which we employ those stereotypes without conscious intervention. This suggests a serious hurdle for any conscious, purposeful intervention that we may design in order to mitigate the socially deleterious effects of negative stereotyping. As Sapolsky argues, at their core, Us/Them responses are not thinking but spontaneous and emotional responses to stimuli. "Stereotyping isn't a case of lazy, short-cutting cognition," he argues, citing the work of David Berreby, "It isn't cognition at all" (Sapolsky 2017, 400). The reflexive nature of our responses leads us to *reason backwards* over our responses and to give them justifications that they really do not have. "Such automaticity generates statements like 'I can't put my finger on why, but it's just wrong when They do that,'" Sapolsky writes, "in such circumstances, cognitions are post hoc justifications for feelings and intuitions, to convince yourself that you have indeed rationally put your finger on why. The automaticity of Us/Them-ing is shown by the speed of the amygdala and insula in making such dichotomies—the brain weighing in affectively precedes conscious awareness, as with subliminal stimuli" (2017, 400–401).

It is most likely the case that attempting to habituate practices in order to give us control over the reflexivity of our response is not possible. It relies on being able to interrupt both processes to which we are cognitively predisposed as well as the troublesome, post hoc justifications that tells us that those responses were, in fact, the right ones to have. Instead, it may be the case that our best efforts will always be defeated by cognitive processes and mechanisms that we cannot control. Testimonial virtue demands that dominant hearers be able to consciously will their way into employing testimonial virtues as often and as consistently as habituating virtue demands—but an epistemic prescription that relies on having this level of conscious diachronic control over automatic cognitive processes, or even backwards-looking, post-hoc justifications, could ever be successful. Consider the case where a dominant knower desires to employ testimonial virtue as a corrective mechanism but has a nonconscious oxytocin response that leads them to having a hostile response to a marginalized knower instead. Can the dominant knower choose to override their neurobiological response in order to respect their "better angels," so to speak? Perhaps, but it is not likely to be the case. To invoke the classic fallacy, our epistemic theories should not ignore the neurobiological *is* in favor of the social and epistemological *ought* simply because we wish it to be that way. Instead, as Sapolsky argues, we need to find the best ways to trick our brains to work in favor of our better selves. "The amygdala typically activates when seeing a face of another race," he claims, "Oxytocin makes us crappy to strangers. Empathy doesn't particularly translate into compassionate acts, nor does refined moral development translate into doing the harder, right thing. There are gene variants that, in particular settings, make you prone toward antisocial acts" (Sapolsky 2017, 614). Still, he argues, we have reasons to believe that we can do better and will be better.

We need to take seriously our propensity for deeply biased and negatively prejudicial perceptions before we reimagining what successful cognitive interventions into testimonial injustice might look like. In chapter 4, I return to the issue of tricking ourselves in order to actualize our better selves. I consider some of the tactics for ameliorating implicit bias and negative prejudice and suggest that, at best, these tactics may only be moderately successfully. Similar to the issue of operationalizing testimonial virtue, the tactics or strategies that we use to inhibit implicit bias should such not rely on knowers trying to consciously *will* their way out of racism, sexism, and other persistent and historical forms of discrimination. As I will suggest in chapter 5, wholesale testimonial justice necessitates that our interventions be primarily *structural* as to avoid relying on the practices and behaviors of individual dominant knowers. Critical for wholesale epistemic justice, the primary goal of this project is to move away from analyses that focus on the epistemic practices and behaviors that dominant knowers can "get right" in order to bring about epistemic justice. Instead, I aim to reorient the focus of discussion toward the following: (1) how testimonial injustice shapes the epistemic practices and behaviors of *marginalized* knowers, and (2) how thinking through these practices and behaviors can help dominant knowers rethink the changes that need to be made in order to bring about a more thoroughgoing epistemic justice. Shifting focus away from dominant knowers and dominant knowing and toward marginalized knowers and marginalized knowing is an act of *centering*. So, and to reiterate, this project is itself a *centering project*. It requires first showing the limitations of the epistemic strategies typically thought to remediate persistent epistemic injustice along with a conceptual expansion of what testimonial injustice looks like from the perspective of marginalized knowing.

In the next chapter, I aim to expand the discussion of testimonial injustice by outlining the epistemic phenomenon and practice of double-knowing, or epistemic labor, as consciously performed by marginalized knowers. My goal is to explain both the practice and the *expectation* of epistemic labor from marginalized knowers on the part of dominant knowers. I go on to argue that in the severe cases epistemic labor a kind of epistemically burdened knowing is produced for marginalized knowers. In these cases, marginalized knowers are forced to knowingly disavow our own epistemic agency when the non-epistemic stakes of making claims of knowledge will result in serious real world harm. Marginalized knowers do not just inhibit ourselves as knowers, we *knowingly* surrender our claim to knowledge (in the context of dominant knowing) in order to avoid harm. The secondary goal of thinking about and thinking through a concept of epistemic labor is that it will help to generate a bidirectional account of testimonial justice that respects the features of marginalized knowing that are often overlooked in the current literature. The hope is to put dominant knowers on better footing when trying to reconceptualize what is required, both theoretically and pragmatically, to remedy testimonial injustice. Lastly, it is important to reiterate that I do not intend to speak for all marginalized knowers, or all marginalized knowing, and that my focus here is primarily on racialized, or race-based, marginalization. Even within that particular framework, there is no monolithic experience shared by all racially marginalized knowers to speak from and there are critical intersections of experience, e.g., race, gender, class, ability, that may not receive the analyses they deserve.

Chapter 2

On Epistemic Labor, Epistemic Disavowal, and Epistemic Burden

In this chapter, I aim to think through the concept of double-knowing, or epistemic labor, as a critical feature of unjust testimonial exchanges. Epistemic labor is a practice of marginalized knowing that involves recognizing the negative stereotypes operating upon us and employing strategies to mitigate those stereotypes in order to gain critical epistemic uptake. (Consider the example of a Black jogger who wears an Ivy League T-shirt in order to minimize the impact hostile of questioning while exercising in a mostly white neighborhood.) Epistemic labor exists on a gradient of clear cases, unclear cases, and cases that straddle the line between the two, or borderline cases. In the first part of this chapter, I consider cases along this gradient in order to delineate, as far as possible, the types of conditions in which epistemic labor is a key testimonial component. I also aim to clarify the relationship between double-knowing as an epistemic phenomenon and epistemic labor as an epistemic practice. I use these terms fairly interchangeably throughout this project and here I seek to isolate how double-knowing functions as a kind of phenomenal "seeing as" while epistemic labor functions as a kind of corollary communicative practice that results from the process of seeing as.

In the second part of this chapter, I go on to consider how double-knowing, or seeing as, can produce a kind of epistemic dissonance for marginalized speakers. Epistemic dissonance occurs when marginalized speakers recognize that the epistemic resources we invoke in a testimonial exchange will not be reciprocally recognized by dominant hearers and, as such, we will need to purposefully *misrepresent* our own beliefs in order to gain epistemic uptake. This is a critical step farther than the type of epistemic labor required in order to mitigate negative stereotypes for the purposes of successful communication. Epistemic dissonance results from the realization that expressing what one believes at a given moment will not only *fail to satisfy* the epistemic expectations of a dominant hearer for non-epistemic reasons, but that "failure to satisfy" will have a very high corresponding non-epistemic cost. Here marginalized speakers find ourselves towing a fine line between who we are as knowers and who the dominant hearer *thinks* we are as knowers. At the end of this chapter, I explore the conditions under which this line collapses and marginalized knowers find it necessary to disavow our capacities as knowers due to fears of severe non-epistemic threat. In these cases, marginalized knowers are in a state of *epistemic disavowal*. Epistemic disavowal is a consequence of extreme testimonial injustice and produces an irreconcilable epistemic burden for marginalized knowers. I address the harm or injustice of this extreme form of epistemic labor as it demands that marginalized knowers must knowingly surrender critical parts of our selfhood for reasons of safety and security.

Clear cases of epistemic labor occur in testimonial exchanges where there is little to no confusion about the operating negative stereotype or its detrimental impact on one's credibility. The introduction to this project introduces a case involving a transgender student at a local college who notices that the gender neutral restrooms are purposefully being neglected by the college custodial staff. The student reports the condition to the buildings and grounds department and is met with disbelief and hostility. They are told that they "must be exaggerating," and "people like you are always stirring things up." In this case, the student recognizes the negative stereotype and identity-prejudicial credibility deficit, adjusts their tone and reframes their initial assertion from a definitive statement ("There has been no toilet paper, soap, or paper towels for 17 days in a row") to a softer, more palatable question for the dominant hearer ("Maybe I'm wrong, but is it possible for someone to take a look at it?"). This is a clear case of epistemic labor because the student recognizes the negative stereotype that is operating upon them and adjusts their assertion in light of this new information. They are compelled to address the dominant hearer's perspective that "people like them" are epistemically untrustworthy in order to determine how to proceed with the testimonial exchange. But this does not mean that the student comes to believe in their own untrustworthiness. Instead they are forced to engage in a temporary, contextual, and highly unstable meaning-making where the negative stereotype remains unchallenged in order to avoid too great a credibility deflation to achieve their non-epistemic end; in this case, the end of having equitably maintained restroom facilities while on campus. Clear cases of epistemic labor are marked by explicitly hostile testimonial environments where the social power of the dominant hearer, coupled with negative stereotyping, makes epistemic labor on the part of the marginalized speaker unavoidable in order to achieve communicative success and practical ends.

In clear cases, marginalized speakers may also *resist* epistemic labor due to the hostility of the testimonial environment. We may verbally insist, provoke, or demand a more just hearing by the dominant hearer in recognition of the fact that we do not expect to receive one without engaging in epistemic labor. For example, if a marginalized speaker reasonably anticipates a testimonial injustice, we may *initiate* a hostile testimonial exchange as a type of provocation and/or form of resistance against perceived injustice. Consider a Black or brown person entering a store only to receive a chilly welcome from a white store clerk. Perhaps we notice that the other all-white patrons of the store have been greeted in a friendly manner by the clerk, with a smile, and the helpful query, "Can I help you with anything today?" We also notice that we are not greeted in such a way or perhaps we are not greeted at all. We are well-aware of ubiquitous negative stereotypes about Black and brown patrons (or "people like you") as deceitful thieves or loud and obnoxious distractions. We may even be habituated to the experience of being followed around shops and stores by suspicious store clerks and regularly queried about our very presence in the store in the first place. In anticipation of an unjust testimonial exchange, we may preemptively and provocatively ask the clerk, "*Do we have problem here?*" This is an example of active resistance to the social and epistemic demand for epistemic labor. Instead of performative displays of excessive politeness or deference—the epistemic tools usually required to gain some initial uptake in these cases—marginalized knowers choose to acknowledge the real epistemic constraints of the environment and respond accordingly. This is because we have been deemed untrustworthy before communication even began.

One might be tempted to argue that marginalized knowers cannot *know* that such situations are epistemically hostile before beginning a testimonial exchange. For example, is it not possible that the white store clerk was simply in a foul mood or tired? Is it possible to know that we will not be believed before we are, well, *not believed?* Could we have an incorrect or inaccurate impression of the epistemic landscape? These are tempting questions to ask. They are tempting questions for the same reasons that it is tempting to question whether an off-color joke is *really* sexist, or a new institutional policy *really* ableist, or a noise complaint *really* racist—such questions demand that socially marginalized knowers prove our own marginalization despite living in social, political, and economic systems that reinforce that marginalization every day. It is asking for proof of our marginalization while the systems and institutions that frame our very existence continue to empirically verify that marginalization in cruel and persistent ways. That is, a sexist joke, ableist policy, or racist complaint *may not be so* in a world without discrimination and marginalization along these axes of social oppression. But that is not the world in which we find ourselves. Epistemic labor is not predicated on marginalized knowers *getting the world right* so much as it predicated on the dominant framework actively and aggressively *getting the world wrong* (and probably willfully so, as I will argue in the next chapter) by denying the ways in which social power gives shape and form to our everyday realities. The need for epistemic labor tracks along the same systems of social injustice and social oppression that systematic testimonial injustice tracks along; the hallmark of such injustices is that marginalized knowers can expect them to occur as *matters of course* not as matters of context.

Patricia Hill Collins uses the term "outsider within" to describe Black women's experiences at the nexus of intersecting forms of discrimination and oppression, i.e., gender, race, and class, and expanded it to capture all unjust social locations that are generated by unequal, and unjust, relations of power (1999, 86). The particular standpoint of the outsider within is characterized by an understanding of the myriad ways in which social oppression and social injustice impact one's life and the lives of others who occupy marginalized social locations. This is coupled with an understanding of the inability (and impossibility?) of full assimilation and/or integration into dominant social spaces. Collins is clear to note that being an outsider within is not a position that applies to an individual identity but to *social groups* that have been subject to historical social injustices. Although it is not the case that all marginalized knowers, or all outsiders within, understand the world as consummate outsiders, still, as Collins writes, "people in outsider-within locations have varying ways of claiming 'outsider within' identities" (1999, 87). The concept of an outsider within runs parallel to the concept of epistemic labor because they both suggest that marginalized knowers understand the forces of social injustice as they act upon our lives and how these forces are founded on unjust social power (there are, of course, degrees of understanding). When I suggest that epistemic labor is not predicated on marginalized knowers "getting the world right," it is to emphasize the inherent conundrum of deciding which perspective, dominant or marginalized, takes priority. Notions of "getting the world right" do not typically begin from the outsider perspective despite compelling reasons to do so.

Epistemic labor shares important similarities to Kristie Dotson's concepts of *testimonial quieting* and *testimonial smothering*. Testimonial quieting occurs when a hearer fails to recognize a speaker as a knower (Dotson 2011, 242). Dotson uses Patricia Hill Collins' discussion of "controlling images" of U.S. Black women as her primary example. Black women are often perceived through a set of negative stereotypes ("mammies, matriarchs, welfare mothers, and/or whores") "which hinders them from being perceived as knowers" (Dotson 2011, 243). Testimonial smothering involves "the truncating of one's own testimony in order to ensure that the testimony contains only content for which one's audience demonstrates testimonial competence" (Dotson 2011, 244). Testimonial smothering, Dotson's argues, "is merely a type of coerced silencing" (2011, 244). Dotson offers an example from Kimberlé Crenshaw about the underreported nature of domestic violence and rape within communities of color. For example, Black women often truncate their testimonies of domestic violence and rape, or self-silence, in order to avoid confirming negative stereotypes about Black male violence (Dotson 2011, 244–245). One of the circumstances that exist in cases of testimonial smothering is that the content of the testimony is deemed "unsafe and risky," as in the risk of conforming to a controlling image or negative stereotype. The other circumstance in cases of testimonial smothering is that hearer(s) "demonstrate testimonial incompetence with respect to the content of the testimony" and that this incompetence follows from "pernicious ignorance" (Dotson 2011, 244).

Like epistemic labor, both testimonial quieting and testimonial smothering can have severe limiting effects on the epistemic practices and behaviors of marginalized speakers. However, in cases of epistemic labor, although marginalized speakers may truncate our testimonies, we may also engage in variety of other practices that range from changing the presentation of our testimony to match the temperament of a dominant hearer, to omitting key components of our testimony (as in the case of testimonial smothering), to producing testimonies that mirror the unjust negative perceptions that are operating upon us, to even abandoning our claim to our own testimony in favor of that of the dominant hearer. In short, epistemic labor constitutes a wider family of epistemic practices, some of which, without suitable context, would not initially appear to be *epistemic* at all, such as adjusting the position of one's body in relation to a dominant hearer or changing aesthetic features of one's appearance. Within the relevant context, these practices or adjustments *do* have epistemic aims and they are performed with the goal of enhancing epistemic uptake.

Whether or not a marginalized speaker chooses to engage in epistemic labor, or strategies to mitigate testimonial injustice, the background conditions of social and epistemic injustice remain woefully intact. It also follows that regardless of whether epistemic labor is useful or necessary in any *particular* exchange, the background conditions of social and epistemic injustice also remain intact. Consider Patricia Williams's now famous "Benetton Story," where she was refused entry into a Benetton store to purchase a sweater for her mother for Christmas (1991, 44–45). Williams recounts the event as follows:

> [O]ne Saturday in 1986[,] I was shopping in Soho and saw in a store window a sweater that I wanted to buy for my mother. I pressed my round brown face to the window and my finger to the buzzer, seeking admittance. A narrow-eyed, white teenager wearing running shoes and feasting on bubble gum glared out, evaluating me for signs that would pit me against the limits of his social understanding. After about five seconds, he mouthed "We're closed," and blew pink

rubber at me. It was two Saturdays before Christmas, at one o'clock in the after-
noon; there were several white people in the store who appeared to be shopping
for things for their mothers. (1991, 44–45)

Now imagine that Williams held up her other shopping bags in the glass window for the store clerk to see, as in to claim, "See? I'm Christmas shopping
as well. I have money too." Or imagine that she attempted to verbally express
her intentions of buying the sweater she saw through the window by pointing
or gesturing despite the store clerk's obvious prejudice. One can also imagine
that none of these strategies would have worked in changing the outcome of
this situation but all are attempts to get the white clerk to extend additional
credibility to Williams and to further consider her implicit request to enter.
This would also be a clear case of epistemic labor. The benefit of extending
Williams's example in this way is that it becomes easier to see the goals of
epistemic labor and to also see the personal and psychic harm it can cause.
In consciously trying to represent oneself in a way that mitigates an operating negative stereotype, an element of *perversion of self* arises. The price of
potential epistemic uptake is, at least in part, having to minimize oneself and
misrepresent what you really believe in favor of whatever expression of belief
is most likely to help you achieve your end—although the end in question
matters a great deal. Engaging in epistemic labor always involves a calcu-
lation of cost and consequence. In Williams's original example, epistemic
labor fails to matter because Williams's own end did not involve getting the
store clerk to allow her into the store after she was denied entrance. Once
the doors of a just testimonial exchange closed, what remained was the sheer
injustice of being publicly denied access to the store and publicly humiliated
due to one's skin color. Understandably, Williams no longer *wanted* to enter
the store. She wanted to scream and yell, to express her rage, and to humili-
ate the store clerk in return (1991, 45–46). She wanted to devalue him as he
devalued her.

As marginalized speakers can refuse to engage in epistemic labor (as in the
Williams example), dominant hearers can also explicitly refuse to engage in
critical uptake of a marginalized speaker's testimony. In the dominant hearers' refusal lies a gray area of unclear cases of epistemic labor. In unclear
cases of epistemic labor, marginalized speakers fail to gain critical epistemic
uptake but it is not clear if it reason for this failure is due to testimonial injustice or due to the social positionality of the hearer. To be clear, unclear cases
of epistemic labor are not cases where the marginalized speaker makes a
mistake regarding the need for labor. As I mentioned earlier, there are important ways in which the marginalized speaker cannot meaningfully fail to "get
the world right" but instead finds instances where the background social
injustices for the hearer *may or may not* be producing the testimonial failure.

The result is an obvious confusion. Take for example the story that Jeanine Weekes Schroer recounts of musician and *The Tonight Show* bandleader, Questlove. Questlove, or Ahmir Thompson, enters the elevator of his New York City apartment building along with a female resident of the building. Upon pressing the button for his floor, Thompson waits for the resident to indicate which button he should push on her behalf. This is a rather common-place and unremarkable feature of sharing both buildings and elevators with other parties. In this case, however, the resident refuses to push a button or indicate the floor on which she lives (Thompson 2013).

To make the resident more comfortable, Thompson ("Six-foot-two, 300 pounds, uncivilized Afro") tries to make his presence and his large body as inoffensive as possible by moving to the back of the elevator and playing games on his smartphone. Next, he politely asks, "What floor, ma'am?" but was met with only silence and fear. As Weekes Schroer describes:

> Questlove is clearly struggling to disconfirm the stereotypes that define him as a dangerous predator. He focuses on signifiers of politeness ("ma'am," "Ladies first," offering assistance); he buries himself in his game to appear uninterested. Of course, because he initially misses the cue that she doesn't want him to know what floor she lives on, he appears extra interested in that information when he inquires again. He has missed aspects of the context that his training in manage-ment of being a black man requires him to notice. He has failed to appear as an innocuous, helpful neighbor as he intended and instead appears suspiciously interested in knowing the location of an apparently vulnerable woman. (2015, 3)

The woman in the elevator was too frightened to engage with Thompson despite his attempts to mitigate negative stereotyping with excessive polite-ness and non-threatening inattention. Thompson's performance of epistemic labor *fails* but it is unclear why this failure occurs. In unclear cases of epis-temic labor, uptake failure may be the result of more than one axis of social oppression operating simultaneously. The complex interplay of credibility and trustworthiness is impacted by the hearer and the speaker existing along different and often incommensurable axes of social oppression. Although we know very little about the woman in the elevator, we can still easily imagine that other social fears and social traumas may be at the root of her response to Thompson. This hypothesis becomes particularly acute considering the prevalence of sexual violence and sexual assault against women in the United States. Because there may be other histories of social injustice and social mar-ginalization at play in this case, it is not clear whether it is negative stereo-typing that is producing the failed epistemic uptake or another form of social marginalization instead. Thompson wonders whether the woman's response is due to her viewing him as a "walking rape nightmare," or whether it is his

Blackness instead, or whether it is both qualities operating in tandem (2013). In either scenario, the inaccessibility of reasons stands out as the primary source of a his unease:

> It kept eating at me (*Well, I guess she never watched the show . . . My English was super clear . . . I called her "ma'am" like I was Webster . . . Those that know you know that you're cool, but you definitely know that you are a walking rape nightmare—right, Ahmir? Of course she was justified in not saying her floor. That was her prerogative! You are kinda scary-looking, I guess?*). It's a bajillion thoughts, all of them self-depreciating voices slowly eating my soul away. But my feelings don't count. I don't know why it's that way. (Thompson 2013)

The ambiguity that constitutes unclear cases of epistemic labor produces the most confusion for marginalized knowers. There is a kind of resignation that accompanies an unjust testimonial exchange that conforms to one's expectation of negative stereotyping and negative identity prejudice but no such resignation is possible when a testimonial exchange fails to conform to expectations. What is left is only a deep skepticism that one can ever render the world correctly.

Thompson takes his failure to "appear as an innocuous, helpful neighbor," as Weekes Schroer describes him, as both his failure and his *burden.* The burden arises out of the demand itself to work to seem as innocuous as possible, to disconfirm negative stereotypes, and to offer an implicit and passive plea to be heard. Although we do have to leave open the possibility that failures of epistemic uptake can be read through different axes of identity, i.e., race, gender, class, ability, etc., and that this may produce incommensurability in understanding, it is also the case that within different intersecting axes of identity there are also issues of identity power (to borrow from Fricker) at play as well.[1] As Collins suggests regarding the concept of an outsider within, a key component of being an "outsider within" is that an individual occupies a social location that has suffered historical injustice and historical social marginalization, or "border spaces occupied by groups of unequal power" (1999, 86). The emphasis here being on belonging to a marginalized social group, not an individually marginalized identity. In the above case, we might consider the social marginalization of women in the United States and the historical prevalence of sexual violence against women as a critical factor in the failed testimonial exchange. The question is: do such considerations help us to better capture what happened in the elevator? The United States also has a violent, painful history of hyper-sexualizing Black men and falsely viewing them as unrepentant sexual perpetrators, particularly in relation to white women. The pervasiveness of this negative stereotype presents a challenge to the first explanation in that it appears to explicitly undermine the gender-based claim, especially in cases where there is "unequal power" at play between socially marginalized knowers.

Unclear cases of epistemic labor will likely involve competing claims of negative stereotyping and thus may be deeply context dependent, falling back on the role that historically-rooted social privilege and social power play in any given context. There is a sense in which unclear cases also lead us into the uncomfortable waters of "oppression Olympics" or debates about which social location, or social group, is more disempowered or disadvantaged in a given situation. While it is tempting to throw up our hands and refuse to engage in such fine-tuned analyses of social power, there are implicit claims and arguments here that must eventually be considered in the broader pursuit of testimonial justice. As I will suggest at the end of this project, dismantling persistent testimonial injustice requires us to get into the weeds and analyze how social power works, and *for whom it works*, and hand-wringing about questions concerning the multilayered nature of oppressed social locations will only serve to further stymie those efforts. The hallmark of unclear cases of epistemic labor is the degree to which different axes of social oppression can operate on a particular testimonial exchange and how that complicates the demand for and receptivity to epistemic labor. Despite their seemingly unresolvable nature, unclear cases are instructive in that they show us how complicated analyzing a testimonial exchanges marked by historically-rooted social oppression can be.

We can contrast the ambiguity of unclear cases of epistemic labor with the inconsistency of borderline cases of epistemic labor. To think through borderline cases, it is helpful to think through the lens of allyship and allyship gone wrong. In the context of social justice, an "ally" is a dominantly-situated individual, institution, or social group who aims to form meaningful relationships with marginally-situated individuals, institutions, or social groups with the goal of social, political, or economic betterment (or inclusion) as determined by those who are marginally-situated. As Rachel McKinnon writes: "[A]llies are generally conceived as dominant group members who work to end prejudice in their personal and professional lives, and relinquish social privileges conferred by their group status through their support of nondominant groups" (2017, 338). I focus on the concept of an ally because allies have good reasons to listen to marginalized speakers, to actively recognize any operating negative stereotypes, and to employ testimonial virtues (as far as they can) to help mitigate any unjust credibility deflations. In short, and at least on the face of things, allies are excellent candidates for the habituation of testimonial virtue because they pledge positive personal and political attitudes toward marginalized speakers. This is not to say that all allies have positive personal and political attitudes toward all marginalized speakers—such non-specificity would water down the value of targeted allyship—but that allies do aim for specific relationships of trust with marginalized individuals or groups such that they ought to make for good sympathetic hearers.

In testimonial exchanges with allies, marginalized speakers generally do not expect the need for epistemic labor. This is because an ally presumably begins from a place of active sympathy or a desire to hear from the marginalized perspective. But this does not mean that problems do not emerge when negative identity prejudice rears its ugly head. Addressing negative identity prejudice can be difficult in the case of allies because they often erroneously believe that they are incapable of prejudice in the first place. Rachel McKinnon argues that such cases can lead to a particularly damaging form of epistemic injustice, *gaslighting*, where a dominant hearer doubts, or fails to believe, a marginalized speaker's testimony because they consider their identity as an ally as making them impervious to prejudice. When allies question the credibility of marginalized speakers, the epistemic harm is a special case of testimonial injustice because "the speaker's moral trust of turning to an 'ally' has been betrayed via the gaslighting" (McKinnon 2017, 342). Allyship and epistemic gaslighting offer an interesting lens through which we can think about borderline cases of epistemic labor because borderline cases are defined by both situational and epistemic *inconsistency*. Meaning that in some instances marginalized speakers are believed and heard and supported while in other instances we are not trusted, deemed non-credible, and maligned. The root of the epistemic injury in the case of gaslighting is that allies invite trust and then cultivate distrust and a similar inconsistency is found in all borderline cases of epistemic labor.

Borderline cases of epistemic labor, unlike unclear cases, do not involve the participants of testimonial exchange belonging to different, or even overlapping, socially oppressed groups. In borderline cases, the social power of the dominant hearer is explicit and the receptivity of the dominant hearer to the testimony of the marginalized speaker is either implicitly or explicitly taken for granted. For example, the dominant hearer might be a friend, teacher, trusted colleague, or friendly neighbor, an individual with whom the marginalized speaker expects a somewhat successful testimonial exchange. What marks these cases as borderline cases is that marginalized knowers cannot tell under which circumstances they will receive an just/unjust hearing by the dominant hearer. Marginalized knowers come to trust the dominant hearer because they have shown themselves to be capable of non-prejudicial hearings in the past—but it is the waxing and waning of their capacity for non-prejudicial hearings that makes the demand for epistemic labor both frustrating and confusing. This waxing and waning behavior also challenges the idea that epistemic "safe spaces" exist within the broader (dominant) epistemic framework. McKinnon is skeptical of the concepts of allies and ally culture because allies are still dominantly-situated knowers and it is too easy for those who are dominantly-situated to default to their own perspective and to deflate the credibility of marginalized knowers as a consequence. This may not always take the form of outright hostility, as in clear cases of epistemic labor, but may happen as a kind of unstated confirmation of the dominant epistemic status quo. That is, a confirmation of a status quo where social power shapes the epistemic landscape of what there is to be known and both gives and retracts epistemic credibility accordingly.

Borderline cases of epistemic labor can also lead to situations where marginalized knowers are compelled not only to change features of our testimony (or the presentation of our testimony) in order to be heard but also to educate dominant hearers who have shown themselves capable of "hearing well" in the past about our own oppression. Nora Berenstain identifies this as a form of "epistemic exploitation" (2016, 570). She offers the example of American actress, Patricia Arquette, and her speech at the 2015 Academy Awards, as a core example of epistemic exploitation. Arquette used her platform at the awards to advocate for pay equity for women, positioning herself as an ally of all women marginalized by rampant pay inequities in the United States. "It's time for us. It's time for women," she claimed, "equal means equal" (Bronner and Gray 2015). Arquette argued that it is indefensible to insist on equal rights for women around the world when women in the United States are still fighting for equal rights at home, particularly in the form of pay equity. Women in the United States have been fighting for other marginalized groups, she concluded, and so now it is time for the *"gay people and people of color that we've all fought for"* to fight for women (Bronner and Gray 2015, my italics). However, as critics and commentators immediately noticed, Arquette distances her advocacy for pay equity away from women in queer communities and communities of color by insisting that *these* communities need to fight for the women, i.e., white women, that have been "fighting for them" in the past. Arquette fails to see the intersection of race and gender in her discussion and, in effect, erases trans women, queer women, and women of color from the category of women also deserving of pay equity.

Criticism of Arquette's speech came from queer writers, writers of color, and writers occupying multiple identities, such as Saeed Jones, Roxane Gay, and Blue Telusma, who were compelled to call out Arquette's error and erasure of marginalized communities of women in the name of a universalized, whitewashed feminism. Berenstain uses the Arquette example to illustrate how dominant knowers often compel marginalized knowers to educate them about our oppression despite being capable of learning themselves. She refers to this as *epistemic exploitation,* or a form of "epistemic oppression marked by the unrecognized, uncompensated, emotionally taxing, coerced epistemic labor" that centers the needs of dominant knowers and exploits that "emotional and cognitive labor" of marginalized knowers (Berenstain 2016, 570).

Berenstain points to Black feminist scholar Brittney Cooper's response to Arquette's speech as an example of a refusal to engage in epistemic labor, as it is neither burden-free nor trauma-free:

> If among feminists, black women are always asked to do the uncompensated labor of educating white women about how they have effed up, is this also not a form of wage inequality? Are these not also the wages of race at play? Some of my academic colleagues of color call this "the black or people of color tax"—the extra, and often unacknowledged labor, time and resources we give to institutions, that our white colleagues don't have to do and for which we are uncompensated, in order to help struggling students of color navigate our institutions and insure diversity at the levels of faculty and administration. If I ramp up my cortisol levels to express my anger and hurt at white women for failing once again to get it, is that not a tax and toll on my health that I pay either in future medical bills or in years unlived? (Berenstain 2016, 572–573)

Cooper suggests that dominant hearers with questions about the types of social oppression that Black women face should avoid asking for education and explanation; instead, she suggests, go ask a white feminist to educate you about the oppression that marginalized people face. To that end, Cooper coined the social media hashtag, #AskAWhiteFeminist, as an act of epistemic resistance to epistemic exploitation and epistemic labor. Even in cases where dominant hearers proclaim themselves allies of the same causes as marginalized speakers, e.g., women's rights, equal pay, we can see that negative identity prejudices and identity-based injustices can still emerge due to dominant knowers defaulting to the dominant status quo. On the face of it, it may seem that examples like the Arquette example only point to the difficulties of seeing or fully understanding social locations outside of one's own. However, as Berenstain argues, justifications of this stripe only serve to further promote the problem of willful ignorance:

> In some cases, the myth that there is a genuine gap in the collective hermeneutical resources is a form of active ignorance that gives the dominantly-situated license to engage in epistemic exploitation. Dominantly situated persons may erase or deny the existence of the relevant hermeneutical resources in question. This is one of the functions of default skepticism in epistemically exploitative exchanges. Pohlhaus (2012: 722) identifies *willful hermeneutical ignorance* as the tendency of the dominantly-situated to dismiss epistemic resources . . . that make sense of experiences and phenomena that are primarily discernible to the marginally-situated . . . Erasing and dismissing these resources allows the dominantly-situated to invoke the pretense that no such hermeneutical resources exist, which in turn supports their position that they cannot and should not be held accountable for their ignorance. (Berenstain 2016, 585)

This type of epistemic mythology can also place marginalized knowers in what Berenstain calls a "double bind," or a testimonial exchange in which marginalized speakers are coerced into epistemic exploitation because of the negative consequences of failing to do so (2016, 576). A double bind transforms borderline cases of epistemic labor into clear cases of epistemic labor because the dominant hearer transforms from a well-meaning, or allied, epistemic position into one that forces a marginalized knower to engage in epistemically exploitative behaviors. Berenstain offers the example of a Black woman being forced to explain to a white male acquaintance the reason a white woman's unwelcome and unsolicited touching of her hair constitutes racist entitlement. The risk of failing to educate and explain herself to her white acquaintance is that he may take her response to the woman as conforming to the negative stereotype, or "controlling image," of the Angry Black Woman (Berenstain 2016, 576). As Cooper claims, this is the "tax" that marginalized knowers often experience in the face of dominant knowing.

Thinking through Berenstain's concept of epistemic exploitation and the double bind offers insight into another aspect of epistemic labor as well. For dominant knowers to hear well they need some understanding of the epistemic resources of marginalized knowers and marginalized knowing. Consider, for example, how the above case would be different if the white male acquaintance knew something about history of objectification of Black women's bodies in the United States and drew upon this knowledge in his response. The call for epistemic exploitation can easily appear to be well-meaning, as in asking questions about the reactions or experiences of marginalized knowers with the desire to learn about marginalized experiences, but it can also be deeply skeptical, as in McKinnon's example of a dominant ally casting doubt about a marginalized knower's experiences of social oppression, prejudice and bias (Berenstain 2016, 571). In both cases, epistemic exploitation involves undue epistemic labor on the part of the marginalized speaker and it makes little difference how the ignorance of the dominant hearer is motivated. I consider epistemic exploitation to be a localized type of epistemic labor where the required labor involves an explanation or education about social marginalization and social oppression. Borderline cases of epistemic labor exists in a space where marginalized knowers can, on occasion, achieve successful testimonial uptake from dominant knowers *without* epistemic labor; however, that success is often marred by dominant knowers skepticism concerning marginalized social experiences coupled with their continued insistence on using only dominant epistemic resources.

In Chapter 3, I take up the issue of dominant knowing and the willful ignorance of dominant knowers. Marginalized knowers are compelled to know and draw upon epistemic resources of dominant knowing *and* marginalized knowing, effectively knowing across hermeneutical divides. Knowing across hermeneutical divides is necessary because *seeing as* a dominant knower and utilizing dominant hermeneutical resources is a critical part of how epistemic labor operates. This is because epistemic labor involves the recognition that one is *not* heard and will not be heard without utilizing different performative strategies and/or without reframing and reshaping the presentation of our beliefs. In extreme cases, the performance or reshaping of our beliefs can make the difference between severe material and bodily consequences or not. I take the idea of *seeing as* from Wittgenstein and the claim that seeing as involves both the description of a perception and an activity of thought: "If you are looking at [an] object, you need not think of it; but you are having the visual experience expressed by the exclamation, and you are also *thinking* of what you see" (2001, 168). The idea is that seeing as is generated both by visual perception and by our background beliefs, concepts, and theories. There is no one wholly accurate description of what is or has been seen, instead, seeing as is interpretative and concept-laden. This concept-ladenness may also explain why marginalized knowers may be better equipped to move between marginalized and dominant perspectives than dominant knowers. Marginalized knowers will most likely have a richer and more detailed conceptual repertoire of both perspectives due our marginalization.

If social marginalization enriches seeing as, then it is equally plausible that social dominance makes the opposite hold true. The *absence* of the necessary concepts will limit the knowers ability to see-as as well. Consider Wittgenstein's triangle example. A knower unfamiliar with the geometric concepts that make up a triangle would find it difficult to see the triangle as a construction of those concepts while a knower who *is* familiar would not: "Clearly the words 'Now I am seeing *this* as the apex' cannot so far mean anything to a learner who has only just met the concepts of apex, base, and so on. – But I do not mean this as an empirical proposition. 'Now he's seeing it like *this*,' 'now like *that*' would only be said of someone *capable* of making certain applications of the figure quite freely" (Wittgenstein 2001, 178). We see what our attention is drawn to, as in the case of Jastrow's duck-rabbit, and we may notice one aspect of perception while failing to notice another. Some things draw us in just as other things do not capture our attention at all. For Wittgenstein, differences in perception may mean very little in most ordinary cases. It may mean the difference between being able to see a stop sign as an octagon in addition to seeing it as a red sign denoting a traffic command. But, he argues, that this *will not* make one knower's description more accurate or more genuine than another's:

> The concept of "seeing" makes a tangled impression. Well, it is tangled—I look at the landscape, my gaze ranges over it, I see all sorts of distinct and indistinct movement; *this* impresses itself sharply on me, *that* is quite hazy. After all, how

completely ragged what we see can appear! And now look at all that can be meant by "description of what is seen." But this just is what is called description of what is seen. There is not *one genuine* proper case of such description—the rest being just vague, something which awaits clarification, or which must just be swept aside as rubbish. (2001, 170–171)

The limitations of this position seem clear in epistemic environments negatively impacted by social power and social hierarchy. Although variation in descriptions of "what is seen" may appear an unimportant consequence of concept-dependent perceptions, the presence or absence of concepts that allow knowers to perceive the world with greater complexity can have serious social and epistemic ramifications. This is because seeing as is *not* a power symmetrical epistemic practice. Marginalized knowers are at a disadvantage because we are compelled to internalize *changes of aspect* and to notice when our epistemic environment demands the framework of dominant knowing and dominant epistemic resources. Perceptions do not only require a knower and the world to be known, they also require that perceptions be *shared* in some meaningful sense in order to achieve other epistemic and material ends. Consider for example a case where two participants in a work incident must report their version of events to human resources personnel. One participant perceives the events as motivated by ableist bias but also knows that human resources routinely ignores such claims and will not act upon their perception of the events. As such, they report a version of events that will be actionable but fails to capture the discriminatory nature of the incident. There are clearly shared epistemic resources at play in this case but that does not mean that invoking those resources is neutral in regard to role of social power. As Patricia Hill Collins writes: "Oppressed groups are frequently placed in the situation of being listened to only if we frame our ideas in the language that is familiar to and comfortable for a dominant group. This requirement often changes the meaning of our ideas and works to elevate the ideas of dominant groups" (2000, vii).

Seeing as also involves epistemic sacrifice on the part of marginalized knowers because it requires that we devalue and deemphasize our own epistemic resources in order to take on "hearable positions" within the dominant framework. It involves the temporary surrender of marginalized epistemologies for the sake of being heard and being able to move about, physically, intellectually, and emotionally, within that framework. For example, in communities of color across the United States, parents and close relations commonly engage in "the talk" or "the conversation" with children and young adults. The talk consists of parents explaining how to handle interactions with police officers, particularly white police officers, and other individuals socially or state-sanctioned to use violence against people of color. Children of color are educated about racism, what to expect during racist interactions, and strategies to stay safe during those interactions. This may include being told to keep your voice respectful (despite being denied respect), to keep your hands in the sight of your perpetrator, to not make sudden movements, and to behave deferentially to any and all authority figures in possession of lethal weapons. This is a straightforward example of marginalized knowers trying to adopt more "hearable" positions in the face of dominant knowing. As with all acts of epistemic labor, this is part social performance and part epistemic reframing, but we can still begin to see more clearly the harm of seeing as, or shifting to, the perspective of the dominant knower. In the case of the talk, children and young adults of color must come to see the world through the lens of both dominant and marginalized knowing, to develop double-consciousness, and this can be a source of both fear and shame.

"When their boys become teenagers, parents must choose whether or not to expose their sons to what it means to be a black man here," Gandbhir and Foster write, "he risks being targeted by the police, simply because of the color of his skin. How should parents impart this information, while maintaining their child's pride and sense of self? How does one teach a child to face dangerous racism and ask him to emerge unscathed?" (2015). One unfortunate result of this process, this constant changing of aspect, is that it can facilitate cases of epistemic dissonance. Epistemic dissonance occurs when marginalized knowers purposefully misrepresent our own beliefs in order to enhance epistemic uptake and avoid harm. With the talk, youth of color must come to know a world that may be hostile to their testimony or may reject it outright due to perceptions of credibility based upon skin color. They must learn to deescalate that hostility, to actively mitigate negative stereotyping, and to implicitly or explicitly plea for more just hearings, e.g., "I am complying," "I can't breathe," without implicating the dominant hearer in any epistemic wrongdoing. This is because such implications can lead to worse material outcomes. The ability to recognize and tool aspect-seeing, to represent yourself *as* yourself, or as the acting stereotype determines, can be life-saving.

Epistemic dissonance, or the active misrepresentation of one's beliefs in order to satisfy the conditions of dominant knowing, fuels the related phenomenon of *epistemic disavowal*. Consider again the case of Kalief Browder from the Introduction. After Browder's suicide, prominent politicians like New York City mayor, Bill de Blasio, and New York governor, Andrew Cuomo, made many promises for criminal justice reform. Such promises included closing the jail complex, Rikers Island, ending pretrial detention for nonviolent offenders, and ending the exploitative "cash bail" system that disproportionately affects lower income communities of color. These are all non-epistemic threats that a young defendant must weigh when what they know to be true is pitted against *what is safe for them to know*. The social cost of "knowing wrong," or failing to make your testimony conform to and/or mitigate negative stereotypes generates all too perfect conditions for epistemic disavowal. Epistemic disavowal occurs when a marginalized speaker is forced to be complicit in their own self-silencing because of severe non-epistemic threat. It is a case that we find too easily when we look into the everyday lives of marginalized knowers. Fear can make facts irrelevant or at the very least socially imprudent. It is often easier for marginalized speakers to assert what dominant hearers want them to know, or to "know wrong," than it is to assert what is true by our own lights. Browder spent three years on Rikers Island because he refused to testify against himself and what he knew to be true about the incident with the backpack on May 15, 2010. Browder was both physically and psychologically tortured on Rikers Island because he failed to willingly surrender his claim to knowledge.

Rachel McKinney argues that social power can unjustly "extract" speech from a knower in a way that harms or wrongs the knower (2016, 259). Unlike cases where speech is constrained by social power, as in the case of silencing or testimonial injustice, "unjust extracted speech," does not prevent speech so much as it *compels it:*

> I take it that silencing, testimonial injustice, testimonial smothering, and discursive injustice all constitute micro-political obstacles to articulation, expression, uptake, and communication. Speakers are rendered communicatively, epistemically, or discursively incapacitated by their interlocutors because of persistent injustice, prejudice, and ideology. As a result, they find their speech unable to do the things they intend and expect it to do. But this is, crucially, not the only significant manifestation of injustice, prejudice, and ideology with regard to speech . . . power does not just keep us from communicating. Power also *gets us* to communicate. (McKinney 2016, 263)

Unjust extracted speech is at the opposite end of the spectrum from epistemic labor. Instead of knowers unjustly working to be heard for non-epistemic reasons, knowers are unjustly coerced into speech for non-epistemic reasons. McKinney considers the Central Park Five case, and the false confessions extracted by police, as the representative case of how power can wrongly compel or coerce speech. Unjust extracted speech is often extracted while a knower is under duress such that they implicate themselves nonconsciously or against their better judgment. But knowers can also *consciously* surrender their claims to knowledge and their position *as* knowers as a form of calculated risk. Consider the serial rapist case that was chronicled in the 2019 Netflix series, *Unbelievable*. The real-life case focused on the events of 18-year-old sexual assault survivor, Marie.[2] Marie reported her rape to the police in Lynnwood, Washington in 2008 but there were inconsistencies in her account. This is a common feature of testimonies of sexual assault due to the impact of trauma, depression, and post-traumatic stress disorder (PTSD) on memory function, but the police were still skeptical of her story.[3] Two of Marie's former foster parents also reported doubts about Marie's credibility: "The two women who had helped raise Marie talked on the phone. Peggy told Shannon she had doubts. Shannon said she did, too. Neither had known Marie to be a liar—to exaggerate, sure, to want attention, sure—but now, both knew they weren't alone in wondering if Marie had made this up" (Miller and Armstrong 2015).

Marie's behavior did not conform to their expectations of the behavior of a rape survivor; Marie was not crying or did not appear to be upset. In fact, they thought that her emotional detachment was a sure sign that she was performing or pretending in order to gain attention like a victim in a *Law and Order* episode (Miller and Armstrong 2015). "That Marie wasn't hysterical, or even upset, made Shannon wonder if Marie was telling the truth," Miller and Armstrong note, "The next day, when Shannon saw Marie at her apartment, her doubts intensified. In the kitchen, when Shannon walked in, Marie didn't meet her gaze . . . In the bedroom, Marie seemed casual, with nothing to suggest that something horrible had happened there . . . And when the two went to buy new bedding—Marie's old bedding having been taken as evidence—Marie became furious when she couldn't find the same set" (2015). The former foster parents conferred and decided to go to the police with their concerns. The skepticism introduced by her former foster parents led the police to turn their investigation to Marie: "Instead of interviewing her as a victim," Miller and Armstrong argue, "they interrogated her as a suspect" (2017). The police pressured Marie to recant her statement. Later, however, she returned to the police station to take back her recanted statement. She knew that she had not lied in her initial account and said that she had been coerced into making a false statement. The police responded by threatening to take away Marie's housing assistance. They also charged her with filing a false police report, making her subject to up to one year in prison. To save her housing, Marie was forced to publicly admit to lying, submit to mental health counseling, and to pay back her court fees. The rapist was later captured with pictures of Marie in his possession. She had been telling the truth.

Marie was compelled to testify against herself as a knower. She surrendered her claim to the knowledge of her own rape in the face of threats of homelessness and a prison sentence. She was compelled to agree with false claims of her own unreliability, her own *lack of credibility*, under threat, and thus disavowed her own capacity as a knower. Epistemic disavowal is the most extreme form of epistemic labor. It involves being coerced into making the type of calculated risk that no individual should have to make, to disavow yourself as a knower due to the material threats and harms that a dominant knower, or dominant institution, puts before you. Epistemic disavowal collapses the line between who a marginalized speaker is as a knower and who a dominant hearer *thinks* a marginalized speaker is as a knower. It is to conform so completely to the negative stereotype operating upon you that you know longer report beliefs as yourself but *as* the stereotype. Miranda Fricker describes this phenomenon in terms of the stereotype *constructing* one's sense of self but that is misleading. What happens in cases of epistemic disavowal is that marginalized knowers determine that "doing as" or "reporting as" the stereotype is the safer bargain. I cannot overstate this critical difference. Knowing oneself as a subject *seen as* an object is quite different than being a subject who psychically collapses into an object. The latter, I would argue, is a characteristic of an extreme psychological state or condition, as in the case of *learned helplessness*, that is arrived at through unimaginable physical and/ or mental abuse, e.g., torture, while the former, although harmful and unjust, does not render a subject's epistemic agency inert. Instead, if the operating stereotype demands that you give testimony as a manipulative liar or face the consequences, then that is what you do. If the operating stereotype demands that you give testimony as an unrepentant criminal or face tougher sentencing, then you may do that as well. This is the reality that *seeing as* reveals to the marginalized knower: determinations of knowledge and truth are mutable and they change in and across dominant and marginalized epistemic spaces.

To reiterate: epistemic disavowal is not equivalent to testimony given under psychological duress, or unjust extracted speech. It does not occur because a marginalized speaker can no longer render the world correctly or make accurate determinations of friend or foe. Epistemic disavowal is the consequence of how social power infects our testimonial exchanges and compels those with lesser power to bend to dominant knowing and the dominant epistemic framework. Epistemic disavowal is both an extreme and *calculated* relinquishing of epistemic agency within the framework of dominant knowing. It is, by its very nature, a last resort in order to avoid serious harm. To recast these cases as examples of marginalized speakers under such duress such that they fail to know or understand their own epistemic behaviors is to deny the severity of the testimonial injustice that solicits the behavior in the first place. Marginalized knowers are often victimized by dominant hearers but we are not unaware of our own victimization. As Charles Mills argues in terms of racial or race-based marginalization:

> These are not cognizers linked by a reciprocal ignorance but rather groups whose respective privilege and subordination tend to produce self-deception, bad faith, evasion, and misrepresentation, on the one hand, and more veridical perceptions, on the other hand. Thus [David Roediger] cites James Weldon

Johnson's remark "colored people of this country know and understand the white people better than the white people know and understand them" (5). Often for their very survival, blacks have been forced to become lay anthropologists, studying the strange culture, customs, and mind-set of the "white tribe" that as such frightening power over them, that in certain time periods can even determine their life or death on a whim. (Mills 2007, 17–18)

Dominant knowers use their social power to externalize wrongdoing, to reorient it onto *the other*, only to later claim that the marginalized speaker "has brought the consequences upon themselves" by choosing their course of actions, e.g., pleading, testifying, confessing, etc. But did Kalief Browder bring the consequences upon himself? Did Marie? In what sense should we understand the word, "choose," in these cases? They did not choose to relinquish their epistemic agency in the sense that "making a choice" often means within the dominant epistemic framework. This is because, for dominant knowers, making choices does not need to bend to any epistemic logic beyond their own. For marginalized knowers, making choices often operates within a much more narrow epistemic space. For example, when Browder refused to testify against himself, or to assert what he knew to be untrue, he made a choice in a criminal justice system that already identified him with criminality, untrustworthiness, and guilt. The framework from which he was compelled to make his choice was and is an *unjust* framework but that does not mean that he was without agency. To deny Browder or Marie epistemic agency would be to disregard what is so distressing about these cases—their commitment to speaking their truth in the face of radical testimonial injustice. It is also why we cannot reduce cases of epistemic disavowal to cases of social power compelling or extracting an unjust testimonial response. Such attempts minimize the harms suffered by marginalized knowers and, more importantly, they minimize acts of epistemic resistance performed in horribly corrupt epistemic environments.

Epistemic disavowal is essentially a form of epistemically *burdened* knowing. The burden comes from having to be accountable to a corrupt dominant framework while simultaneously being a victim of that very same framework. It is unclear what type of remediation measures would be necessary to correct for such abhorrent and inexcusable epistemic wrongs. What does seem clear is that remediation cannot begin without thinking through the ways in which social power generates entire ways of knowing that perpetrate and reinforce testimonial injustice while simultaneously demanding epistemic labor. Entire epistemologies are predicated on maintaining social power and social dominance and de-emphasizing the social and epistemic impact of marginalization and oppression. Dominant knowing is shaped by these forces and often willfully refuses to acknowledge the world as seen through the eyes of marginalized knowers. But as we can see, this refusal is not power symmetrical. Marginalized knowers come to see and to know the world through the eyes of dominant knowers while our own ways of knowing go ignored. This reinforces deep hermeneutical divides between dominant and marginalized knowers and makes epistemic remediation appear a far off goal absent some way of bridging these divides such that dominant knowers come to speak and to *hear* across difference.

NOTES

1. My analysis of this case as an unclear case of epistemic labor is not equivalent to the claim that the experience described by Questlove fails to be an instance of racial prejudice. I do not intend to discount or discredit first person testimony of racial prejudice or invoke what Rachel McKinnon refers to as the "epistemic injustice circle (of hell)" (2017, 340). I claim instead that much of the non-verbal aspects of this case make an epistemic analysis of *epistemic labor* very complex without further information. The woman's refusal to let her floor be known can be read in myriad ways that both do *and* do not implicate her as holding racist beliefs. We can contrast this case with the case of the store employee in that the situational factors, i.e., in a public space, with by-standers, with minimal fear of bodily threat, etc., allow for a more clear reading of the failed/resistant testimonial uptake. That is, the situational factors are not nearly as loaded with *both* racialized and gendered understandings of the epistemic environment. Unclear cases of epistemic labor are often cases that are muddied by what goes *unspoken* in loaded contexts. They can, in a very real sense, be read both ways despite the fact that there may be a "truth of the matter."

2. Marie's real name was redacted in the newspapers due to the heightened publicity of the case and her desire to preserve her anonymity; in the press, she is commonly referred to by her middle name instead.

3. Jenkins et al. researched whether rape survivors with post-traumatic stress disorder (PTSD), or PTSD, and without comorbid conditions, such as alcohol abuse and substance abuse, suffered from impaired memory function at similar rates as combat veterans with post-traumatic stress disorder (PTSD). The study found that rape survivors with post-traumatic stress disorder (PTSD) suffered from impaired memory function at similar rates as combat veterans, concluding that memory deficits are most likely associated with a post-traumatic stress disorder (PTSD) diagnosis: "post-traumatic stress disorder (PTSD)-positive subjects without comorbid alcohol abuse have impaired free recall. This is similar to the results reported for veteran groups (5, 6, 8). Compared to normative standards for age and education, one-third of the post-traumatic stress disorder (PTSD)-positive group fell at least two standard deviations below the mean for delayed free recall; fewer than 5 percent of the members of the other two groups were this impaired. Overall, the post-traumatic stress disorder (PTSD)-positive group scored in the mild to moderately impaired range when compared to normative standards" (Jenkins et al. 1998, 279).

Chapter 3

Hermeneutical Marginalization and Willful Hermeneutical Ignorance

In the last chapter, I went through the three case types of epistemic labor and considered what happens when epistemic labor, in its most extreme form, leads to epistemic dissonance and epistemic disavowal, the conscious surrender of one's claim to knowledge. Cases of epistemic disavowal are severe cases of epistemic labor where "knowing wrong," or actively failing to conform to the negative stereotype operating upon you, leaves marginalized speakers vulnerable to a variety of negative social consequences. Knowing wrong is rooted in the framework of dominant knowing. Thus the question that this chapter takes up is whether dominant knowers should be epistemically responsible for the negative consequence of dominant knowing. There are at least two ways of considering this question. One way, articulated by Miranda Fricker, involves thinking about the negative consequences of dominant knowing as belonging to a category of non-culpable hermeneutical injustices that result from gaps or flaws in collective hermeneutical resources. Another way of looking at this question involves thinking about whether "collective hermeneutical resources" sufficiently includes the co-existing epistemic resources of marginalized knowers and asks whether dominant knowers are responsible for knowing and employing *those* resources in addition their own. In this second sense, there is greater conceptual room for individual culpability and individual failure of epistemic responsibility because the failure to know and employ marginalized epistemic resources captures both an *external failure*, as in compelling marginalized speakers to conform to negative stereotypes, and an *internal failure*, as in failing to recognize flaws or gaps in dominant epistemic resources.

This chapter has two broad goals. First, I consider Fricker's argument for hermeneutical injustice rooted in hermeneutical marginalization.

Hermeneutical injustice occurs when, due to unequal participation in shared meaning-making, there are gaps or flaws in collective hermeneutical resources. These gaps harm knowers although they do not harm them equally. Knowers on the losing end of structural identity prejudice are less likely to be able to contribute to shared meaning-making and thus are less likely to have their social experiences reflected in collective hermeneutical resources. This creates a structural prejudice in collective hermeneutical resources where the absence of critical social concepts may render unintelligible important features of marginalized social experiences. At the extreme end, Fricker argues, this may even include concepts that provide an understanding of oneself. "The primary harm of hermeneutical injustice, then, is to be understood not only in terms of the subject's being unfairly disadvantaged by some collective hermeneutical lacuna, but also in terms of the very construction (constitutive and/or causal) of social identity," she argues, "In certain contexts, hermeneutical injustice can mean that someone is socially constituted as, and perhaps even caused to be, something they are not" (Fricker 2006, 107). Although hermeneutical injustice finds no individual culprit, as, according to Fricker, it is structural prejudice and structural phenomenon, it still rests with dominant knowers to *extend* credibility to marginalized knowers when they suspect that successful epistemic uptake is impeded due to hermeneutical marginalization (Fricker 2007, 170).

I question Fricker's argument for hermeneutical marginalization and thus the grounds for her conception of hermeneutical injustice. Thinking alongside a series of critiques offered by Rebecca Mason, José Medina, Gaile Pohlhaus, Jr., and others, I argue, instead, that hermeneutical marginalization is better understood as the failure of dominant knowers to learn and use marginalized epistemic resources and ways of meaning-making. The dominant epistemic framework refuses to engage with a variety of marginalized epistemic resources and thus testimonies of marginalized knowers often fail to be understood. That is, what looks like hermeneutical marginalization may really be a case of willful ignorance. Unlike Fricker's analysis, I take for granted that hermeneutical injustice due to structural identity prejudice does ethically and epistemically implicate the individual dominant knowers who comprise those structures in wrongful or willfully ignorant knowing. Thus I consider the question of whether dominant knowers should be held responsible for failing to know and/or failing to use marginalized epistemic resources as a way of remedying what is most likely *motivated* hermeneutical marginalization. I also suggest that although it may be tempting to think of willful ignorance as a matter of degree, or existing on a continuum, between cases of *not needing to know* and *needing not to know,* historical social oppression against marginalized knowers is so ubiquitous, and the opportunity to know so easily accessible, that failing to know is really tantamount to *actively not knowing.*

Hermeneutical injustice is a type of structural epistemic injustice that results from absences or gaps in collective hermeneutical resources. These gaps are critically connected to the unequal distribution of social power and how that social power allows for the structuring of shared hermeneutical resources. "If you have material power," Fricker claims, "then you will tend to have an influence in those practices by which social meanings are generated" (2007, 147). Gaps in social meaning can affect both those who benefit from such gaps and those who do not, but it is those without social power who are most vulnerable to their effects. Fricker centers her analysis around two examples: postpartum depression and sexual harassment. In the first example, Fricker recounts a case from Susan Brownmiller's book on the American women's liberation movement. The case tells the story of Wendy Sanford and her experiences at a consciousness-raising event on the MIT campus in late 1960s. Sanford discovered that her experiences of depression and isolation after the birth of her child had a name, *postpartum depression*. The naming of her experience helped Sanford to realize that the condition for which she blamed herself was not an individual or personal defect but a psychological and physiological diagnosis that was beyond her control. Fricker describes Sanford's discovery at the women's group as a "hermeneutical breakthrough" that allowed her and others to overcome the hermeneutical injustice of having a critical experience veiled from understanding (2007, 149). Fricker argues that the veiling of this important post-birth experience prevented Sanford and other women from fully realizing themselves in their capacity as knowers.

Marginalized knowers are vulnerable to hermeneutical injustices because there are gaps where "the name of a distinctive social experience should be" (Fricker 2007, 150). They are not able to call on collective hermeneutical resources to make sense of their experiences because they do not have sufficient social power to create and/or structure those resources or sufficient power to engage in social meaning-making. For Fricker, this leads to a kind of hermeneutical wrong or harm where there is no agent singularly responsible for that harm. Instead, it shifts the question of culpability to society in general and the issue of remediation to those who most suffer hermeneutical marginalization. We can see the scope of this point in Fricker's second example, again drawn from the work of Susan Brownmiller, of the sexual harassment of Carmita Wood. Wood served as the administrative assistant of Cornell University physicist, Boyce McDaniel, for eight years through the late-1960s and mid-1970s. During those years, Wood was subjected to inappropriate and aggressive touching, kissing, and sexual innuendo from McDaniel, e.g., rubbing and jiggling his crotch near her desk, brushing against her breasts, and pinning her in an elevator to kiss her. The stress of the job gave Wood chronic back and neck pain and she quit as a result and filed for unemployment insurance. Wood described her reasons for quitting as "health-related" because there was no clear way to describe her experiences of sexual harassment. The New York State Department of Labor insisted that Wood's reasons failed to qualify as health-related and recategorized her reasons as "personal" and "non-compelling"; subsequently denying of her unemployment insurance claim (Strebeigh 2009, 222).

Wood's case was found by Cornell University women's group, Working Women United, a women's consciousness-raising group organized and led by professors Lin Farley, Susan Meyer, and Karen Sauvigné. Many of the women who attended the women's group shared similar experiences of what later came to be known as "sexual harassment" as well as how they had been forced to leave jobs for reasons similar to Wood's reasons. The group helped Wood find a lawyer to appeal her insurance decision and organized a "speak-out" in order to coalesce and name their collective experiences as a group. What was the right name for the experience of sexual violation, objectification, and *risk* that so many women shared? What was the best way to tie these experiences together under one term or one heading?

> Sauvigné reports, "we decided that we also had to hold a speak-out in order to break the silence about this." The "this" they were going to break the silence about had no name. "Eight of us were sitting in an office of Human Affairs," Sauvigné remembers, "brainstorming about what we were going to write on the posters for our speak-out. We were referring to it as "sexual intimidation," "sexual coercion," "sexual exploitation on the job." None of those names seemed quite right. We wanted something that embraced a whole range of subtle and unsubtle persistent behaviors. Somebody came up with "harassment." Sexual harassment! Instantly we agreed. That's what it was. (Fricker 2007, 150)

The momentum of the movement led to hearings on "women and work" before the New York City Commission on Human Rights and to articles in the *New York Times* on the newly coined sexual harassment (Brownmiller and Alexander 1992). In the midst of these events, Wood lost her appeal for unemployment insurance. However, her story was a catalyst for sexual harassment claims from women across the United States. The women's group established an institute to capture new inquiries from women, match women with lawyers, and work on new policies focused on Title VII and sex discrimination:

> Things had begun to percolate on the legal front. Working with a large map and color-coded push-pins, Sauvigné and Meyer matched up complainants with volunteer lawyers and crisis counselors. Initially, aggrieved women sought redress by filing claims for unemployment insurance after they'd quit their jobs under duress, or by bringing their complaints to local human rights commissions. Ultimately the most important means of redress became the EEOC, the federal

agency charged with investigating and mediating discrimination cases under Title VII of the 1964 Civil Rights Act. (The inclusion of sex discrimination in the 1964 act had been introduced at the last minute in an attempt to defeat the bill.) (Brownmiller and Alexander 1992)

A critical takeaway from the case of Carmita Wood (and others at the time) is that many women *knew* sexual harassment before the term "sexual harassment" was named as an actionable form of sex discrimination under the law. The ability of the Farley, Meyer, and Sauvigné to mobilize so many women and so many claims of sexual harassment is a testament to that reality. It was another women's problem without a name brought to life through the organization of feminist women. "We didn't have the phrase sexual harassment until I was in my 40s," Gloria Steinem famously stated, "it was just called 'life'" (Gandhi 2019). Sexual harassment became a new concept both socially and legally by the mid-1970s but the *experiences* of sexual harassment (or "life") clearly predated that formal naming.

Fricker describes the absence of a collective term for sexual harassment and the process of naming sexual harassment as an example of women not being able to *understand* their own experiences (or make their experiences self-intelligible). As in the case of Wendy Sanford, the lack of a collective term for sexual harassment is intended to indicate an unjust conceptual hole in our collective hermeneutical resources constituting a structural epistemic injustice against women as knowers. If we consider the lack self-intelligibility as Fricker describes it, then it is easy to see the harm of hermeneutical injustice. Hermeneutical injustice requires us to imagine that entire parts of ourselves and our experiences may be unknowable to us because we do not have the conceptual language to make sense of those experiences. There is a kind of epistemic terror and loneliness that unwrites this concept. One can imagine the relief—the physical and psychic relief—of finally being able to make sense of what was once hidden from you. The problem with this characterization of hermeneutical injustice is that it is not clear that such unknowability of experience exists for any individual knower. If it *does* exist, then it is not clear that the unknowability will be sufficiently divorced from the repertoire of *other* shared and related concepts such that the entire experience will be shielded from self-knowledge *or* from sharing with others.

Consider that in the above example the women's group was still able to invoke several shared concepts of what was happening to them before landing on the concept of sexual harassment. That is, they were very much engaged in sense-making and meaning-making within a localized space that eventually became a social concept and legal concept that was more broadly shared. This aligns with Fricker's original characterization of hermeneutical marginalization. In in the earliest moments, the women's consciousness-raising group was able to discuss a variety of stories sufficiently self-categorized as "something wrong," or "bad behavior," before the speak-out and before their collective experiences were labeled as sexual harassment. In the same way that it is possible to feel and describe the symptoms of a mysterious illness before the illness is named or given diagnostic criteria, it is also possible to feel and describe the symptoms of an unnamed social behavior before it is named and given diagnostic criteria. Naming our collective or shared experiences can help us put broader and more amorphous descriptions under one conceptual umbrella. It can also give us a shared language with which to focus and orient our collective discussions and social-political agendas. However, and I emphasize, all of this can be true but that does not mean that we have no way of making sense of our experiences without the conventions of social naming:

> Although Wood may not have gleaned the broad significance of her experiences—for instance, that it was a widespread and unfortunately common occurrence in many women's lives—her actions following her denied unemployment insurance claim betray Fricker's description of her as someone who failed to understand . . . Wood sought out feminist Lin Farley, voluntarily shared her experiences of workplace maltreatment with Farley's consciousness-raising group, and helped organize and participate in a speak-out on the topic . . . These were not the actions of a woman mystified by her experiences of a yet-to-be-named phenomenon. (Mason 2011, 297)

Consider again the example of Wendy Sanford and her discovery of the term, postpartum depression. Fricker's argument is that Sanford's failure to understand her postpartum depression was the due to the fact that it was poorly understood socially and thus impossible for her to make self-intelligible. Sanford's interaction with the consciousness-raising group allowed her to see her own experiences for what they were and to give those experiences a proper name. The argument being that it was the *naming* that allowed for self-intelligibility. There are two things that seem to complicate this characterization. First, Sanford experienced symptoms of postpartum depression despite having no clear conceptual box in which to put those symptoms. Her experiences, as nameless as they may have been, were not without language sufficient enough to share those experiences with others and to be understood. It is not clear that *naming* made her experiences self-intelligible or rather than naming allowing her to coalesce her experiences in way that could be more easily shared and discussed. The latter explanation seems the better explanation if only because it does not require us to deny some basic luminosity to our own mental states. To deny Sanford the self-intelligibility of her experiences is to link the naming of an experience to *having* an experience in way that seems difficult to defend.

Second, names and experiences do not always align into simple or unique relationships of understanding. Sometimes names capture a broad range of experiences and sometimes a broad range of experiences cannot be neatly captured by a name. In the process of communication, we are often doing interpretative work. We can see this in terms of the experiences that fall under the conceptual and diagnostic umbrella of postpartum depression. The name "postpartum depression" is way of capturing a wide range of depressive symptoms that arise for women post-birth, symptoms that include anxiety, insomnia, mood swings, irritability, difficulty bonding, and suicidal thoughts, and others. In the mid-1970s, there was no unique criteria for determining postpartum depression according to the *Diagnostic and Statistical Manual of Mental Disorders*, or *DSM-III*, and there is no unique criteria for determining it today. Instead, postpartum depression exists under the broader conceptual framework of depressive disorders and mood disorders and is determined primarily by way of a differential diagnosis. Thus the name, "postpartum depression," does not pick out a unique set of symptoms or experiences, lay or otherwise, but instead relies on a speaker being able to sensibly communicate their experiences to a hearer, e.g., friends, family, healthcare professionals, and the hearer being able to decode those experiences as pertaining to (or not) the relevant name. If we consider the Sanford example from the point of view of the women's group, or from the point of view of testimonial *hearers*, then we can see this point more clearly. Sanford had to understand her own experiences well enough to communicate those experiences to a group, and in turn, the group had to understand Sanford's testimony well enough to match those experiences to a name.

It is reasonable to conclude that Sanford's experiences were sufficiently *content-rich* by her own lights such that the women's group was easily able to understand and categorize her experiences as postpartum depression. Additionally, the activity of having her experiences affirmed by a social group and given a social name allowed Sanford to see her experiences—the ones she had been blaming herself for—as *socially important* and not based upon personal failures. Naming can be critically important for a shared understanding of a particular phenomenon and a shared understanding may, in turn, help marginalized knowers to align their personal experiences with the broader social world. What is not clear is that it is the social world that helps us to render our experiences intelligible *to ourselves* instead of confirming that our individual experiences can and *should* take up and make up social space. The larger issue that emerges from Fricker's discussion of hermeneutical injustice is the question of *whose* experiences are affirmed in shared social spaces and whose experiences get to make up hermeneutical repertoires? That is, whose experiences count such that they can be added to what we are calling *collective* hermeneutical resources?

I emphasize the word "collective" because of how it can obfuscate the role that social power plays in the creation, adoption, and maintenance of hermeneutical resources. The notion that there are, or can be, collective hermeneutical resources de-emphasizes the myriad ways in which marginalized knowers create and maintain epistemic resources for ourselves and engage in shared meaning-making in ways that may not, and often do not, intersect with collective (dominant) epistemic resources and dominant ways of meaning-making. There is a critical overlap between the hermeneutical resources that dominant knowers create and employ and the collective hermeneutical resources that all knowers are called upon to employ for both epistemic reasons, i.e., to successfully communicate and to be understood, and for non-epistemic reasons, e.g., to be perceived as credible, to avoid the material consequences of being misunderstood. Thus when considering the issue of hermeneutical injustice and unjust hermeneutical gaps, it is also important to consider how those hermeneutical gaps may only exist for those who take dominant hermeneutical resources *as* collective hermeneutical resources. Rebecca Mason argues:

> Fricker's understanding of "collective" hermeneutical resources thus glosses over important distinctions—in particular, distinctions between dominant and non-dominant hermeneutical resources—that bear on how we interpret hermeneutical lacunae. A gap in dominant hermeneutical resources with respect to one's social experiences does not necessitate a corresponding gap in non-dominant hermeneutical resources. For instance, although dominant hermeneutical discourses were deficient with respect to women's experiences of sexual harassment, this did not mean that non-dominant hermeneutical discourses—those discourses that generated and were generated by the twentieth-century women's movement—failed to provide women with the interpretative resources to understand and articulate their experiences of it. Certainly, when dominant discourses of interpretation neglect the experiences of marginalized groups, members of those groups suffer some injustice. However, because marginalized subjects may have non-dominant hermeneutical resources to draw upon in order to interpret their social experiences, gaps in dominant hermeneutical resources do not necessarily result in hermeneutical injustice. (2011, 300)

Framed in another way, gaps in dominant hermeneutical resources may also be instances where dominant knowers *actively* refuse to recognize and engage with the hermeneutical resources of marginalized knowers. That is, dominant knowers give little to no consideration to the existence of marginalized epistemologies and thus act as though their own hermeneutical resources extend to marginalized knowers as well. Nora Berenstain argues that Fricker's account of hermeneutical injustice—and particularly her use of Carmita Wood as the paradigmatic example—constitutes an instance of failing to know or recognize the hermeneutical resources created and used by women of color.

Because Fricker fails to recognize histories of epistemic resistance to sexual harassment by women of color, she engages in an insidious form of *structural gaslighting* where the epistemic resources of Black women, in particular, are downplayed and omitted by appealing to notions of the collectivity of resources. Berenstain argues that Fricker whitewashes the history of sexual harassment in order to preserve the wrongful idea that it was white feminists who made sexual harassment socially intelligible, and *self-intelligible,* to women of color. Furthermore, she claims, willful ignorance allowed Fricker to ignore the parts of Susan Brownmiller's work that highlighted women of color as being on the frontlines of resistance to sexual harassment (as many of the first litigants were Black women) (Berenstain 2020). The argument that dominant knowers, including Fricker, refuse to recognize or engage with marginalized hermeneutical resources has been articulated repeatedly in relation to discussions of hermeneutical injustice. José Medina argues that Fricker should be careful not to theorize a kind of universal unintelligibility with regard to collective hermeneutical resources that fails to account for the question of for whom those resources are in fact unintelligible:

> We should be careful not to tie too closely people's hermeneutical capacities to the repertoire of readily available terms and coined concepts, as if oppressed subjects did not have ways of expressing their suffering well before such articulations were available . . . I find it problematic that Fricker operates with the working assumption that when there is a hermeneutical gap, a range of experiences will be rendered unintelligible *for everybody* independently of particular communicative dynamics. To begin with, the unintelligibility of an experience in the speaker's terms is quite different when the speaker's attempts to communicate the experience encounter inattention, hermeneutical neglect, or hermeneutical incapacity—that is, when the interlocutors are unmoved or unable to identify what is being talked about—and, on the other hand, when speakers encounter *counter-interpretations* that systematically distort their communicative attempts—for example, when a woman's attempts to convey that she feels sexually harassed are interpreted as an overreaction to "harmless flirting." Systematic distortions of this sort typically limit some subjects' capacity to understand under some conditions, but not of the whole social body. As epistemologies of ignorance have emphasized, it is not always the case that hermeneutical gaps render experiences unintelligible for everybody equally and in every communicative dynamic. (2012, 98–101)

Marginalized speakers' experiences may appear unintelligible to dominant hearers in cases where their default position is to accept dominant hermeneutical resources as collective hermeneutical resources. Instances of unintelligibility may prove the rule in testimonial exchanges between marginalized knowers and dominant knowers due to the role that social power plays in

shaping and enforcing the use of dominant hermeneutical resources. If marginalized knowers draw upon epistemic resources outside of the framework
of dominant knowing, we are put into the position of *knowing wrong,* or
having our testimony deemed as untrustworthy or non-credible by dominant knowers. This is also part of how epistemic labor is compelled by the
dominant framework. Failing to make ourselves heard within the dominant
framework often means that we are not heard at all. The consequences of
such failures are not purely epistemic, if they were, then the results might
not be so socially significant. A world marked by persistent confusion and
incommensurable reports of experience would be an odd world but perhaps
not a harmful one. The problem is that the consequences of failing to "know
right" or "know correctly" within the dominant framework are often *material*
consequences that impact marginalized knowers' ability to move through the
world without undue burden or unjust obstacles. Making ourselves intelligible is often a matter of combating dominant knowers' refusals to engage
with marginalized hermeneutical resources and their active ignorance of how
social power dictates the consistent use of dominant hermeneutical resources.

Medina, invoking Charles Mills, considers *white ignorance* as one of the
most pervasive examples of active ignorance, an ignorance that insists on its
own invisibility. "White ignorance," Medina argues, "is a prime example of
active ignorance, which is the kind of recalcitrant, self-protecting ignorance
that builds around itself an entire system of resistances" (2012, 213). Fricker
attempts to differentiate critiques of hermeneutical injustice from the charge
of white ignorance arguing that white ignorance "names a certain kind of
individual or collective *motivated cognitive bias* in what evidence and/or
social interpretations relatively privileged groups attend to and/or integrate
into the rest of their beliefs and deliberations" and this motivated bias is both
wrongful and epistemically blameworthy (2013, 50). Hermeneutical injustice, on the other hand, is meant to denote a category of experience where
hermeneutical marginalization makes parts of a knower's experiences unintelligible for epistemically non-culpable reasons. Although Fricker concedes
that there may be *motivated* or ideologically enforced hermeneutical gaps,
she wants to leave room for hermeneutical gaps that are not due to socially
powerful and privileged interests *making those gaps.* Instead, she claims,
there are hermeneutical gaps that result from of other, more neutral social
forces that lead to hermeneutical marginalization and offers the example of
1960s teenagers trying to explain the social and political importance of rock
music to conservative parents (one imagines something like birth of "mods"
from The Who's *Quadrophenia*). This seemingly neutral example is revealing
in that it highlights what is the heart of Fricker's disagreement with Mason,
Berenstain, Medina, and others. Fricker assumes that it is possible to pick
out historical moments and their respective knowers from a neutral social

backdrop without *de facto* affirming the resources of some groups, i.e., dominant knowers, and omitting or de-emphasizing the resources of other groups, i.e., marginalized knowers.

However, the presumption of a universal landscape of meaning-making appears to be, in the face of so much evidence to the contrary, another form of willful or motivated ignorance. This is because the presumption of neutrality flattens the historical and sociopolitical conditions under which social concepts and social meanings are made. As Berenstain argues, this is a whitewashing form of willful ignorance that refuses to see marginalized knowers *as knowers* who have built and maintained robust epistemologies of resistance to (and despite) the dominant status quo. White ignorance stands out as a form of active ignorance because of its insistence on the *neutrality* of its worldview and because of the perverse relation of epistemic dependence it can force upon marginalized knowers ("the 'white' in 'white ignorance,'" Mills argues, "does not mean that it has to be confined *to* white people") (Mills 2007, 22). This dependence may be difficult to see if white ignorance is thought of as Fricker describes it: "epistemic practices that are *wrongful and epistemically culpable*, owing to some epistemic fault or vice such as wishful thinking, denial, self-interested selectiveness as regards the evidence, suppression of historical context, and so on" (2013, 49–50). In her estimation, white ignorance is a problem at the level of belief, an epistemic vice at the *doxastic level*, and not a problem inherent to social meaning-making in general. For Fricker, it is not that the racist knower does not have access to the relevant social concepts to correct their beliefs but that they fail to use the available social concepts in a socially and epistemically responsible manner:

> In the case of the straightforward racist's white ignorance there is no hermeneutical lacuna, indeed no poverty *of concepts* at all, for the white racist's ignorance is not caused by any lack of conceptual-interpretive resources. Let all the hermeneutical resources stand available to him, what he lacks is the epistemic self-discipline to apply the extant resources in an epistemically responsible way so as to achieve cognitive contact with reality. (2013, 51)

The case of the racist knower stands distinct from the non-racist knower who merely lacks access to the relevant social concepts. In the latter case, Fricker argues, white ignorance would not be epistemically culpable. The non-racist knower suffers from the social suppression of the relevant social concepts due to structural flaws in the collective hermeneutical resources. The knower misunderstands his own social experiences but not through any fault of his own. Fricker suggests that conceiving of white ignorance in this way best combines the concept of white ignorance with hermeneutical injustice while preserving her original understanding of the concept. This is because, in the opposite case, the case where the necessary social concepts are omitted from collective hermeneutical resources for racist ideological reasons, white knowers would not be disadvantaged by these omissions but privileged by them. Thus, she argues, it would be odd to think of the resulting white ignorance as a type of hermeneutical injustice *against* white knowers. Still, Fricker's argument seems to stubbornly miss the point. The point is that her characterization of hermeneutical injustice assumes that collective hermeneutical resources are (or can be) created without gendered, racist, ableist ideologies actively factoring into their making from the start. Mills points out that the boundaries of the debate become clear once we take seriously the claim that the creation and use of collective (dominant) hermeneutical resources are bound together with histories of social and political oppression. As such, epistemic oppression— or in Fricker's terms, hermeneutical marginalization—should not be cashed out in terms of the *access* to social meaning-making but in terms of how collective (dominant) hermeneutical resources mirror and reproduce systems of domination and oppression. In this sense, collective hermeneutical resources, as Fricker understands them, operate in tandem with unjust systems of social power and it is by way of that power that collective hermeneutical resources are created and reproduced. Medina's claim that white ignorance is a form of hermeneutical injustice becomes all the more clear when considered in this way. This is because *racist ideology* has warped the hermeneutical resources that all knowers share. Mills writes of Medina's argument:

> Medina is not saying that white ignorance is a hermeneutical injustice for *whites*, but for nonwhites trying to advance alternative views. As Rebecca Mason (2011) has pointed out, Fricker's notion of "collective hermeneutical resources" blurs the distinction between (in my formulation, not hers) the resources of *G1* ideology and the collective resources that *would* be available were it not for *G1* domination and suppression of *G2* subordinate counter-hegemonic alternatives, in part because Fricker underestimates the extent to which such counter-hegemonic *G2* ideation is possible. But once such "subversive" cognition is conceded, the "conflictual" (as against "cooperative") assumptions of non-ideal theory undercut "symmetrical" framings. While the social-structural prerequisites of hermeneutical injustice stipulated by Fricker must be differentiated from the clearly interest-based conceptions of injustices resulting directly from individual denial, bad faith, etc., it is still the case that the "structure" functions overall to reproduce *G1* domination, and that although individual members of *G1* are not responsible for its reproduction, *G1s* as a group are complicit with it. So insofar as white ignorance functions to suppress emancipatory alternatives, injustice is being done to people of color. (Mills 2013, 42)

Insisting that hermeneutical injustice, and subsequent hermeneutical marginalization, are distinct epistemic phenomena from white ignorance does not allow us to hone in on the ways in which dominant knowers are epistemi-cally responsible for creating and maintaining unjust epistemic environments. It also does not allow us to sufficiently problematize the social meanings, meaning-making practices, and hermeneutical resources that knowers are compelled to share because of how the machinations of social power operate. Fricker maintains that, although there may be localized hermeneutical prac-tices and marginalized hermeneutical resources, there still exists a relatively unproblematic shared pool of hermeneutical resources that contain "meanings that just about anyone can draw upon" (2016, 163–167). However, and this is critical to point out, shared meanings and collective hermeneutical resources are historically *made* not found. They do not appear from ahistorical nothing-ness. As such, hermeneutical marginalization is most likely the result of *how* those social meanings have been historically made and *for whom* those mean-ings are meant to address. Hermeneutical marginalization is not the result of a generic social powerlessness, it is the result of how dominant hermeneutical resources have been constructed to create and *exploit* that powerlessness in the first place. There are powerful, and often violent, histories of marginal-ized knowers (with our "localized hermeneutical practices") trying to enter *our meanings* and *our concepts* into the dominant framework of shared social meanings with little success, and this lack of success is not by consequence but by design.

Consider the fight to enfranchise the Black American vote in the southern United States and the fight against discriminatory poll taxes, literary tests, and "grandfather clauses" for voting. Despite protests, appealing to the press, and vast pamphleteering campaigns, Black voters call to fully exercise voting rights, and rights of full citizenship, failed to be heard for almost a hundred years after the ratification of the Fifteenth Amendment. Black Americans have tried for over a century—and are *still* trying—to enter our social experi-ences, our meanings, into the dominant framework of American citizenhood. Is our failure to be heard within the dominant framework a result of our relative social powerlessness? Or is the dominant framework constructed to ensure our social powerlessness such that we cannot be heard? Fricker seems to argue for the former case but this argument requires ignoring how social power, and *whiteness* in particular, operate in ways that make mar-ginalization appear an unfortunate historical consequence and not a *method* of socio-structural design. In essence, it insists on the colorblindness of the machinations of history. As Mills writes:

> If previously whites were color demarcated as biologically and/or cultur-ally unequal and superior, now through a strategic "color blindness" they are assimilated as putative equals to the status and situation of nonwhites on terms that negate the need for measures to repair the inequities of the past. *So white*

normativity manifests itself in a white refusal to recognize the long history of
structural discrimination that has left whites with the differential resources they
have today, and all of its consequent advantages in negotiating opportunity
structures. If originally whiteness was race, then now it is racelessness, an equal
status and a common history in which all have shared, with white privilege
being conceptually erased. (Mills 2007, 27–28, my italics)

Mills notes how cognitive psychologists commonly distinguish between
"cold" and "hot" mechanisms of cognitive distortion or mechanisms "attrib-
utable to intrinsic processing difficulties and those involving motivational
factors" (2007, 34). There is no conflict in assuming that one can *choose* not
to know what is in one's interest not to know. This type of cognitive distortion, or choosing not to know, is a critical part of white social identity in the
United States. Mills describes this as a type of *motivated irrationality* and a
critical component of white social identity in the United States. Instead, and
in the name of colorblindness, white social identity reinforces itself through
what it willfully and consistently fails to know about itself ("the convenient
amnesia about the past and its legacy in the present") (Mills 2007, 35).
Beneficiaries of socially oppressive epistemologies may never see themselves
as illegitimate heirs to beliefs that reinforce their dominance; and obligors,
those bound and othered by oppressive belief systems, may never be able to
destabilize epistemic systems that are dependent upon their social oppression.
Mills describes this as a kind of *naturalization of oppression* where systems
of domination and oppression are so internalized by white knowers as to be
practically invisible:

> Nonwhites then find that race is, paradoxically, both everywhere and nowhere,
> structuring their lives but not formally recognized in political/moral theory. But
> in a racially structured polity, the only people who can find it psychologically
> possible to deny the centrality of race are those who are racially privileged, for
> whom race is invisible precisely because the world is structured around them,
> whiteness as the ground against which the figures of other races—those who,
> unlike us, are raced—appear. The fish does not see the water, and whites do not
> see the racial nature of a white polity because it is natural to them, the element
> in which they move. (Mills 1997, 76)

To be clear, however, white knowers have an *interest* in not knowing about
racial privilege. They also have an interest in not knowing how that privilege
constructs the wider world of social meaning. Fricker describes this kind of
privilege, or willful not-knowing, as an epistemic wrong that is *not quite on*
purpose: "The interesting thing about denial, or other kinds of motivated or
willful ignorance or non-knowing, is of course that it is not quite on purpose,
or not in the normal conscious way" (2017, 130). However, Pohlhaus argues,

although there may be little to compel dominant knowers to investigate how their privilege impacts the creation and maintenance of hermeneutical resources, it is not impossible for them to do so. The refusal to engage with marginalized epistemic resources may be difficult to overcome but "such a refusal is not an inherent inability, but rather a willful act" (Pohlhaus 2012, 729). For Pohlhaus, knowers are situated in terms of how their social position relates to the prevailing hermeneutical resources of the time as well as how their social position impacts the creation of those resources: "situatedness may be suited to the epistemic resources that prevail in a given society or may not, depending upon whether the experiences that arise from one's situatedness influence the development of epistemic resources" (2012, 717). "*What* one knows because of situatedness," she claims, "is not the same as *whether* and *how* one is able to know through the use of epistemic resources" (Pohlhaus 2012, 718). The extent to which our epistemic resources make sense of the world, and make sense of our social experiences, is directly related to the extent to which those resources are *interdependent*. To consider epistemic resources truly interdependent, or truly *collective* epistemic resources, those resources need to equitably include the social concepts and social meanings of all knowers.

If dominant knowers create and maintain hermeneutical resources that attend to their social experiences while omitting or willfully ignoring the epistemic resources of marginalized knowers, then there are critical parts of the world of which they will not be able to make sense. Learning and using marginalized epistemic resources can "call one's attention to whole parts of the world that were previously not obvious at all" but this requires that dominant knowers not *willfully ignore* those resources in the first place (Pohlhaus 2012, 722). There are clearly parts of our collective social experiences for which dominant epistemic resources are not at all useful, Pohlhaus argues, and this should lead dominant knowers take an active interest in attending to those parts of the world (2012, 720). The failure to attend to marginalized epistemic resources is tied to the role that social power—and racial privilege in racially stratified societies—plays in the control and implementation of dominant epistemic resources. To maintain social power, it can be useful to deny, or willfully fail to understand, social concepts that might challenge the legitimacy of that power: "When a group with material power is vested in ignoring certain parts of the world, they can, therefore, maintain their ignorance by refusing to recognize and by actively undermining any newly generated epistemic resource that attends to those parts of the world that they are vested in ignoring" (Pohlhaus 2012, 728).

We can see how this work in cases where dominant knowers call in to question, or outright dismiss, critical social concepts like "white privilege," "date rape," and "heteronormativity" (Pohlhaus 2012, 722). Similar to other epistemologies of ignorance, like white ignorance, the refusal to engage with marginalized epistemic resources is often rendered invisible by those with social power by way of a willful not-knowing. Because having social power allows you to shape the wider epistemic landscape by reinforcing certain social meanings and social concepts while denying or ignoring others, the role of willful ignorance is obscured by what is not said, or not acknowledged, or not reproduced in the production of social meanings. For Pohlhaus, the refusal to engage with marginalized epistemic resources, and the insistence on interpreting the world as though marginalized resources do not exist, constitutes a specific category of epistemic injustice called, *willful hermeneutical ignorance.* In cases of willful hermeneutical ignorance, dominant knowers choose to misunderstand, or *actively not know*, the parts of our collective social experiences that require marginalized epistemic resources in order to understand. That is, willful hermeneutical ignorance shields dominant knowers from critical parts of the social world.

As in standpoint theory, taking an interest in the lives of marginalized others is part of developing a critical standpoint from which know better and to know with greater objectivity. Pohlhaus, emphasizes, citing Sandra Harding, that dominant knowers compound their willful ignorance by refusing to take an interest in the lives of marginalized others. Instead, they take too much comfort, and too great of an interest, in the narrow scope of their own worldviews. "Ignorance is not something to which one is doomed because of social position," Pohlhaus, concludes, "but rather something one chooses to maintain" (2012, 731). This interpretation of willful ignorance is not quite equivalent to the "not quite on purpose" characterization offered above by Fricker. *Not quite on purpose* suggests a kind of naive, non-culpable ignorance on the part of dominant knowers and untethers them from the structural creation and maintenance of the social concepts dominant in the wider epistemic landscape. Her interpretation fails to capture how individual not-knowing goes hand-in-hand with the dominant social refusal to see social and epistemic equity as a necessary component of a shared understanding of the social world. Most acutely, it fails to hold individual dominant knowers to account for their not-knowing and asks us to take their naivety—their "commonplace" failure—as a justifiable reason for not taking an interest in the lives of marginalized others. The question is, at what point does failing to know, or failing to take an interest in the lives of others, becomes an epistemically culpable behavior?

In other work, I have attempted to carve out the difference between magnitudes of willful ignorance in order to capture the type of "willful ignorance as naive non-knowing" that Fricker describes (Posey 2021). It is far too much of an overreach to take all non-knowing as culpable –as Mills notes, there are many facts about the natural and social world that dominant knowers do not know, or hold mistaken beliefs about—but it is also far too lax to assume that only *active self-deception* is epistemically culpable. There are clearly some beliefs about the natural and social world that unfortunately converge with beliefs that underwrite and reinforce social injustice and social oppression and it is these beliefs that we are trying to capture. A spectrum may exist between something like Fricker's conception of "epistemic bad luck" and what Medina refers to as "ignorance out of luxury"; in the latter case, because a dominant knower "does not need to know," they, in fact, do not know due to a kind of "epistemic laziness" (2007, 152; 2013, 34). In cases of epistemic bad luck, the necessary epistemic resources are unavailable, as in not yet generated, or not sufficiently widespread, such that there is a hermeneutical gap where a concept should exist. For the reasons noted earlier in this chapter, this idea seems plausible at the level of concepts but implausible at the level of experience. That is, while there may be gaps in naming due to insufficient naming conventions and/or socially-christened terminologies, it is difficult to imagine that this creates unintelligibility at the level of individual experience. This is further complicated by the idea that any alleged unintelligibility must also account for histories of social marginalization, alternative epistemic resources, and marginalized epistemologies that *can* explain those experiences.

On a revised spectrum, we find something like Medina's idea of "not needing to know," or *epistemic laziness* born out of default epistemic privilege on one end of the spectrum (2013, 33–34). This *not needing to know* describes a dominant knower who is socially, politically, and epistemically comfortable, a knower who is epistemically incurious, but whose lack of curiosity is not motivated by denial. Consider a young, white, cisgender American teacher at a religious postsecondary institution who is surprised to learn about physical assaults on trans, non-binary, and gender non-conforming students at her institution. She is worried and concerned about the assaults but she is not curious enough to learn about how systemic violence and bullying impacts marginalized students in educational environments and in the wider social landscape. The teacher fails to learn something critical to understanding the individual cases of violence and bullying that she comes across, or may come across, in her daily experiences. She is not *hiding* from herself, epistemically speaking, and she is not in denial. She is untroubled and incurious about the lives of marginalized others. This does not mean that she shows no care or concern for the harms suffered by individual students. It means that she does not see the harms suffered by her students as importantly connected to the histories of social-historical harms and social-historical injustices suffered by LGBTQAI+ communities. Her epistemic laziness stems from her social and epistemic privilege in relation to her students such that it appears as though she *does not need to know* about systemic violence and bullying in LGBTQAI+ communities in order to make sense of her own lived experiences.

At the other end of this spectrum, we find a kind of "needing not to know" that requires "an enormous amount of effort to be hidden and ignored" (Medina 2013, 34). The idea of *needing not to know* aligns with what Kristie Dotson calls "contributory injustice," where dominant knowers rest comfortably in their willful ignorance despite the fact that there are alternative hermeneutical resources that they could use instead of "structurally prejudiced hermeneutical resources" (2012, 32). This is willful ignorance in its most problematic, malignant form. It does not rest on the dominant knower "pretending not to know" what they very well know about marginalized epistemic resources but on a kind of willful cognitive maneuvering where dominant knowers refuse to make what they *do* know—that marginalized epistemic resources exist, for example—consistent with their own worldview. The difference is that *pretending* is primarily performative, it is about making something appear as such, whereas willful ignorance is primarily about denial, or about being unwilling to call something to mind or to admit its existence. Willful ignorance in its malignant form constitutes a culpable denial, *an active disavowal,* of the epistemic resources of marginalized knowers:

> To borrow from Slavoj Žižek, such disavowal is fetishistic and compulsive in its demand to "know but not know," and can be seen in the myriad ways in which some dominant knowers cognitively maneuver to keep the homogeneity of their worldview intact. In some cases, extending credibility to marginalized epistemic resources would generate a worldview so altered and disjointed that any epistemic adjustments would result in a violent cognitive schism. This, I take it, is the epistemic position that generates the most vicious forms of racism, sexism, homophobia, and transphobia. As James Baldwin so aptly describes in *The Fire Next Time*, such knowers are "mad victims of their own brainwashing (1993, 102)". (Posey 2021)

But how far apart are these two conceptions of willful ignorance? Medina suggests that habitual epistemic laziness transforms into willful ignorance if the lack of epistemic curiosity atrophies a dominant knower's cognitive attitudes (2013, 33–34). Consistently taking an interest in the lives of others is surely difficult work, and it does seem, at least at first glance, that we need some way of capturing the kind of failure of attention to the lives of marginalized others that is involved in *not needing to know*. But when we stop to consider that our social experiences are riddled with historical patterns of violence and aggression against marginalized communities, it is hard to imagine that these patterns can be ignored without some serious cognitive effort. In environments of racialized willful ignorance, or white ignorance, it may be easier to see how this works because racism (at least in the historical-colonial patterns of the West) is so pervasive. In the case of the United States, from American slavery, to the three-fifths compromise, the Civil War and Reconstruction, Jim Crow and "Separate but Equal," the Civil Rights era, Black Liberation to Black Lives Matter, histories of racial violence and racial oppression are inseparable parts of American history. Failing to take an interest in the history and consequences of racism would be to fail to take an interest in the most important factors that gives shape to our collective social lives. It results, as Pohlhaus claims, in dominant knowers failing to make sense of critical features of their own social experiences.

Cases of *not needing to know* often collapse into cases of *needing not to know* because the evidence needed in order to know, and to take interest, is so deeply intertwined with the lives of dominant knowers. That is, the evidence of racial marginalization and racial oppression is everywhere and impacts almost every element of American social life, including work, housing, education, social organization, and political association. Evidence of racial marginalization and racial oppression is so ubiquitous that failing to recognize it has been described as a kind of motivated cognitive bias that infects every aspect of knowing. Robin DiAngelo describes this motivated bias of white knowers as "white fragility." White fragility runs parallel to aversive racism, or implicit bias and prejudice, and describes the lack of "psychosocial stamina" or "racial stamina" to recognize, evaluate, and/or understand the role of whiteness in race-based oppression (DiAngelo 2011, 56). DiAngelo argues, also echoing Mills, that white knowers are socialized to see whiteness as a neutral, objective position from which "otherness" stems, not as a social location founded on and maintained by implicit and explicit beliefs about white superiority and white supremacy. White fragility, she argues, is "the *sociology of dominance*" (DiAngelo 2018, 113). This makes talking about race and racial marginalization a fraught endeavor for white knowers as there are powerful reasons why not seeing, not knowing, and not taking an interest in the lives of marginalized others, serves as a protective mechanism. It means that white knowers—as a dominant collective—can feel absolved from active or passive failures to know better.

Instead dominant knowers often hold onto versions of history that obscure patterns of violence and oppression, rewriting and reimagining history absent the role social power plays in constructing unjust social and epistemic environments. DiAngelo argues that the power to neutralize (and sanitize) the past is a feature of social dominance and, specifically, of white privilege. It allows dominant knowers to be incredulous about claims of social and epistemic injustice while willfully ignoring how past histories have given rise to both dominant *and* marginalized knowing. The resulting presumption is that social and epistemic inequality emerged ahistorical and without clear cause. As DiAngelo writes:

> As a white person, I can openly and unabashedly reminisce about "the good old days." Romanticized recollections of the past and calls for a return to former ways are a function of white privilege, *which manifests itself in the ability to remain oblivious to our racial history.* Claiming that the past was socially better than the present is also a hallmark of white supremacy. Consider any period in the past from the perspective of people of color: 246 years of brutal enslavement; the rape of black women for the pleasure of white men and to produce more enslaved workers; the selling off of black children; the attempted genocide of Indigenous people, Indian removal acts, and reservations; indentured servitude, lynching, and mob violence; sharecropping, Chinese exclusion laws; Japanese American internment; Jim Crow laws of mandatory segregation; black codes; bans on black jury service; bans on voting; imprisoning people for unpaid work; medical sterilization and experimentation; employment discrimination; educational discrimination; inferior schools; biased laws and policing practices; redlining and subprime mortgages; mass incarceration; racist media representation; cultural erasures, attacks, and mockery; untold and perverted historical accounts, and you can see how a romanticized past is strictly a white construct. But it is a powerful construct because it calls out to a deeply internalized sense of superiority and entitlement. (2018, 59, *my italics*)

The kind of willful ignorance required to support a position like *not needing to know* seems untenable when not needing to know rests upon the denial of one's own dominant social location. Although DiAngelo claims that those occupying dominant social locations are socialized not to see their own socialization, this "not seeing" is not equivalent with not knowing. Instead it is an active, willful, failure to know about marginalized others that is intrinsically tied to a willful failure to know oneself as well. In a public lecture, DiAngelo explains this obliviousness to racial oppression and racial marginalization as kind of fundamental irrationality in the vein of Žižek's fetishistic disavowal; it materializes as *"I know very well, but . . . "* where dominant knowers acknowledge white supremacist ideology as shaping their everyday affairs but invoke that very same ideology as a tool of justification:

> There's a stew inside of white people that makes us really irrational on this topic and I've tried to identify some of those pieces, but one of them is that we really are taught not to see this, so if you're a person of color scratching your head thinking, "How can they not see this? Like, I just don't believe that they don't see this." We actually really don't see it, oh, and hell yes, we know it, and we do see it, but we cannot admit that. It's [that] both [of] these things are actually true. We don't see it. And we do see it. And we can't admit to it. And it's part of what makes us so irrational. (Seattle Channel 2018)

In some ways, DiAngelo's explanation brings us back full circle to our initial question about how to hold dominant knowers accountable for failing to know and failing to take an interest in the lives of marginalized others. DiAngelo suggests that the fundamental irrationality at the heart of willful ignorance may best be understood as an irrationality at the level of *scrutiny* and not at the level of belief. That is, dominant knowers do not hold inconsistent and thus irrational beliefs about marginalized knowers (e.g., "I find people of color credible," "I don't find people of color credible"); rather, they refuse to hold the beliefs that they do have about marginalized knowers to sufficient epistemic scrutiny. This often entails holding beliefs about marginalized knowers based upon little to no evidence and/or retreating from evaluating evidence that contradicts entrenched beliefs about their own racial and social superiority. Hence, dominant knowers hold on to unjustified beliefs about marginalized knowers as well as unjustified beliefs about *themselves*. The avoidance of epistemic scrutiny exposes the *fragility* of beliefs as these beliefs are accepted and maintained with little regard for evidence. Fragile beliefs are ultimately corrupt at two levels: at the level of individual belief and the level of our collective social lives. This is because fragile beliefs, or beliefs that cannot withstand epistemic stress or scrutiny, can still produce and hostile social and epistemic environments.

Consider now that a problematic theoretical situation has emerged. In my attempts to conceptualize the degree to which dominant knowers should be held responsible for the negative consequences of dominant knowing, I have arrived at the conclusion that they should be responsible for their willful ignorance and their epistemically fragile beliefs. Willful ignorance, in many respects, is the fuel that drives testimonial injustice and epistemic labor—and benign forms of ignorance fare no better than malignant forms. Benign willful ignorance, or ignorance that stems from epistemic laziness, or *not needing to know,* is disingenuous in cases where it is motivated by entrenched beliefs about one's own social superiority, and this may capture most, if not all, benign cases. The desire to maintain social superiority compels dominant knowers—and white knowers, as a core example—to ignore easily available evidence about how histories of social dominance and oppression create and corrupt the epistemic landscape. Although this critique primarily describes cases of racialized willful ignorance, it may very well extend to any social location rooted in histories of social dominance and social oppression and/ or predicated on ideas of naturalized or essentialized social superiority. That said, if dominant knowers are responsible for willful ignorance and epistemically fragile beliefs, then we will need posit some method or mechanism by which they can resolve them.

Notice, however, that there is a tension between the charge of willful ignorance and claims made in Chapter 1 about the negatively biased nature of our spontaneous and nonconscious perceptions. If willful ignorance is itself fueled by nonconscious perceptions and implicit biases and prejudices, then we have arrived at a layer of analysis where it is difficult, if not impossible, to ask dominant knowers to be more epistemically responsible. The presumption is that implicit bias and prejudice will lead dominant knowers to turn their attention away from the parts of the social world pertaining to marginalized knowers and marginalized knowing, and if that is the case, then dominant knowers cannot be said to be *willfully* ignorant in any meaningful sense. Rather, they fail to know because they cannot adequately attune themselves to the lives of marginalized others. I think, however, that this is not the best way to unpack the issue of implicit bias and prejudice. Willful ignorance describes a feature of active non-knowing that encapsulates both marginalized knowing *and* dominant knowing. It does not merely describe *attention to marginalized others* as an epistemic good but as a good critically inseparable from an adequate knowledge of oneself and one's social environment. The crux of Pohlhaus's argument is that dominant knowers willfully failing to know marginalized epistemic resources is also about them failing to know *themselves* and the real shape of the epistemic terrain. While implicit bias might prejudicially skew knowing about marginalized epistemic resources, it neither precludes knowing them or makes it unimportant for the dominant knower.

Consider an example extrapolated from the case, *EEOC v. Premier Operator Services*, where Mexican-American workers won an Equal Employment Opportunity Commission, or EEOC, claim after being targeted by English-only policies on the job. In this example, Spanish-speaking workers, targeted by similar policies, use language (or what the court calls, languages of "national origin minorities") as an epistemic resource by which to gather evidence of discrimination.[1] Most EEOC claims against English-only policies pertain to charges of *disparate impact*, or policies that are facially neutral but discriminatory in practice. The U.S. courts do not have a good history of ruling in favor of disparate impact claims so the workers strategize using a different tactic. They judge that they are more likely to win a *harassment* claim than a discrimination claim and so decide to repeatedly and excessively use Spanish-English cognate terms in conversation, e.g., *infracción, violación,* whenever the supervisor visits the factory floor. Thrown off by the cognates, the supervisor continues to write up the workers for violating policy and threatens termination. The workers, having used cognates, now have a case against the supervisor: they file a claim for being harassed for speaking *accented English*. The workers have utilized language as a marginalized epistemic resources in order to address their unfair treatment at work. Although language does not immediately stand out as a marginalized epistemic resource, it is clearly so in cases where language is connected to socially marginalized identities.

In the factory case, even if the initial policy resulted from implicit bias, it still would have been beneficial for the dominantly situated supervisor to know what was going on with the workers. He was, instead, willfully ignorant about a social experience of which he was a *key participant*. As Pohlhaus argues, willful ignorance makes it such that the dominant knower does not know even what is *in his interest* to know and implicit bias may have minimal influence over the reasons for that ignorance. Consider a related case where a white waitress holds implicit biases about Chinese-Americans patrons. She is routinely rude and dismissive to Chinese-American patrons and receives numerous complaints about her behavior. However, as her job is not in jeopardy, she finds no immediate reasons to question herself. Instead, she dismisses the complaints as something that "people like them" do in social spaces. She notices, after some time, that her tips from Chinese-American patrons are far less generous than those given to her workmates. She does not understand the cause of the disparity and sets out to learn about Chinese culture in the United States with the hope of learning something that can increase her tips. She stumbles across information about histories of discrimination against Chinese immigrants, and, feeling bad, promises herself that she will go out of her way to be nicer to her patrons. She has, by default, temporarily interrupted her implicit bias while *still failing to understand* critical features of her social environment. This is because she does not know how her biases—and biases like hers from other dominant knowers—contribute to the social and epistemic realities that Chinese-Americans (who are, of course, *not* necessarily Chinese immigrants) face.

This is all to say that implicit bias and willful ignorance come apart in many ways. We can address willful ignorance, and thus rampant epistemic injustice, without resolving the issue of implicit bias and prejudice. Although, as I consider in Chapter 4, resolving willful ignorance may be *easier* with the self-regulation of implicit bias as we are more likely to have successful discussions across hermeneutical divides if dominant knowers can prevent implicit bias from tainting testimonial exchanges. In Chapter 4, I begin to think about what successful discussions across divides might look like, starting through the lens of the epistemology of disagreement. Disagreement, on its face, should bring dominant knowers in concert with marginalized knowers in ways that make hermeneutical differences explicit. In these cases, disagreement should also make dominant knowers less confident in their beliefs about marginalized knowing and marginalized epistemic resources. The problem, however, is that disagreement is also likely to be tainted by implicit bias and prejudice such that credibility deflations cannot be avoided. I consider whether implicit bias can be controlled at its source, or consciously self-regulated, by dominant knowers using targeted regulation strategies. The goal is to make both testimony and disagreement less biased such that *better discussions* across hermeneutical divides are possible. However, if less biased discussions are not possible, then what remedies are left to deal with willful ignorance? In the second half of Chapter 4, I think through what I call, *evolving epistemic frameworks*. Evolving epistemic framework are temporary social-epistemic spaces created by dominant knowers and marginalized knowers in order to amplifying marginalized epistemic resources. These frameworks rely on dominant knowers' explicit recognition of both bias and willful ignorance coupled with the desire to cede public social and epistemic space to marginalized knowers. The resulting frameworks are highly unstable spaces for collective meaning-making that rely temporary transfers of social power and epistemic power in order to operate.

NOTE

1. EEOC v. Premier Operator Services, Inc., 113 F.Supp.2d 1066 (N.D. Tex. , 2000).

Chapter 4

Disagreement, Implicit Bias Interventions, and Evolving Epistemic Frameworks

I begin this chapter by looking at how to interrupt willful ignorance. The goal is to understand how dominant knowers and marginalized knowers can engage in meaningful collective discussions about what the landscape of shared meaning-making could look like—its boundaries, its conceptual limitations, and around whose epistemic resources we ought to focus—without reducing marginalized knowers to negative stereotypes and deflating our credibility in the process. The end of collective discussion is, with hope, a better idea of what epistemic remediation for epistemic injustice should look like along with a way to begin dismantling the hegemony of dominant knowing. I start this process by thinking through the lens of the epistemology of disagreement. This is because disagreement itself ought to motivate dominant knowers to consider that their beliefs about marginalized knowers, and marginalized epistemic resources, might be poorly justified. I consider what happens in cases where the disagreeing parties are epistemic equals, or epistemic peers, and cases where one party is an epistemic inferior and the other an epistemic superior. I consider also how disagreement is impacted by unjust deflations of credibility due to negatively prejudicial assignments of epistemic inferiority. Here I return to the discussion in chapter 1 about the role that implicit bias and prejudice play in assignments of credibility. Following Jennifer Saul, I consider the potential for dominant knowers' self-regulation of implicit bias, in the name of better and more productive disagreements, by way of four model types: (1) strategy models, (2) discrepancy models, (3) Implicit Association Test (IAT) models, and (4) egalitarian goal models. I argue that these models are flawed as self-regulatory mechanisms and that it may be the case that consistent self-regulation of implicit bias, like consistent applications of testimonial virtue, is not a viable goal.

In the second part of this chapter, I try to unpack the following problematic: implicit bias and negative stereotyping have deleterious effects on marginalized testimony, both by unjustly deflating credibility and by demanding epistemic labor. As I suggested in chapter 1, it may well be the case that we cannot interrupt testimonial injustice by asking dominant knowers develop sensibilities and sensitivities to the testimony of marginalized knowers. Negative stereotyping may prove too cognitively compelling to be overwritten by applications of testimonial virtue. As I try to show here, this may *also* be the case for conscious strategies to mitigate implicit bias. That is, at the level of individual agents, our cognitive predispositions toward biased and prejudicial perceptions are perhaps too "sticky" for lasting, diachronic intervention. Although nothing too serious hangs on this point being proven wrong—as it will just lead to better epistemic outcomes for marginalized knowers—much more hangs on it being right. Thus something needs to be said about how we can think about epistemic responsibility (and epistemic *remediation*) for testimonial injustice and epistemic labor in the situation where such interventions are not really possible. In this case, I think it is useful to look into the world for examples of social-epistemic spaces where collective meanings are made by dominant knowers and marginalized knowers, and where these first-order problems, i.e., implicit bias, negative stereotyping, are explicitly entertained as *impediments* to better and more just knowing. Here I consider the example of the Never Again movement, arising from the 2018 school shooting in Parkland, Florida, as bringing together dominant and marginalized knowers with such goals in mind.

As I suggested in the last chapter, I think it best to uncouple first-order issues of implicit bias and negative stereotyping from the *second-order issue* of willful ignorance. This is because willful ignorance does not rely on implicit bias or negative stereotyping to get off the ground. Willful ignorance can be resolved by entirely self-interested desires on the part of dominant knowers to understand marginalized knowers (and marginalized knowing) in order to better understand themselves and their social environment. In nobler or more sympathetic cases, dominant knowers can also address willful ignorance on the grounds of allyship or as a means of rejecting the hegemony of dominant knowing. In these cases, willful ignorance may be easier to interrupt and easier to remedy. Dominant knowers may not be able to "hear well," as in hear without bias or prejudice, but they can still choose to understand how their dominant social location distorts the epistemic landscape for themselves and for other knowers. I call examples like the Parkland, Florida example, *evolving epistemic frameworks*. In evolving epistemic frameworks, dominant knowers can choose to temporarily renounce their epistemic privilege and amplify the speech of marginalized knowers with the hope that selective silence and speech amplification will make explicit the epistemic resources of marginalized knowing. Dominant knowers may also come to serve as *epistemic allies* for marginalized knowers with the goal of extending epistemic credibility to marginalized epistemic resources.

However, as welcome as evolving epistemic frameworks are, they are still temporary spaces of collective meaning-making and knowledge-production. They are *charitable epistemic acts* on the part of dominant knowers and are thus is highly unstable in terms of challenging the dominant status quo. As I will argue in chapter 5, epistemic charity fails to provide sufficient motivation for dominant knowers' long-term adoption and/or employment of marginalized epistemic resources and is thus an imperfect solution for epistemic remediation of epistemic injustice. This is because extensions of epistemic charity do not meaningfully challenge the social and political power structures upon which dominant knowing is predicated. As such, they cannot offer *lasting* solutions for persistent testimonial injustice and epistemic labor. Still, evolving epistemic frameworks offer opportunities for addressing and interrupting willful ignorance as well as opportunities for pursuing meaningful hermeneutical disagreement about how socially divided epistemic resources can lead to truly collective hermeneutical resources.

David Christensen claims that disagreement fills a critical gap in how we arrive at and justify our beliefs. He writes: "We live in states of epistemic imperfection because we do not always respond to the evidence we have in the best way. Given that our epistemic condition consists in imperfect responses to incomplete evidence, part of being rational involves taking account of these sources of imperfection" (2007, 187). The good news, he claims, is that disagreement can help us improve upon our own epistemic imperfections. Disagreement, or *doxastic* disagreement, can beneficially challenge our current beliefs (or credence/degree of belief in a given P, if we are Bayesians) such that we revise our beliefs in light of the outcome of the disagreement. Consider a case where two friends are on a road trip to Boston but have found themselves lost on an unmarked service road. The friends consult the same road map and have the same background knowledge of the geographical area but they do not reach the same conclusion about which local road to take in order to find the main highway. What should they do in this situation? Let's assume that one friend believes, "Taking Evergreen Road to the highway will be faster," while the other friend believes, "Taking Quarry Road to the highway will be faster." In this case, the friends are also *epistemic peers*; that is, they regard each other as equally capable of adequately evaluating and analyzing the evidence before them. They also consider each other to be reliable testifiers. Thus it would be reasonable for them to both employ something like the *Principle of Indifference* where they assign an equal degree of belief between each possible outcome, concluding that the outcome of taking either route would be equally successful.

We can complicate this scenario by disallowing what Christensen calls, citing Adam Elga, a "live-and-let-live" attitude toward the two outcomes and assuming that there is something else at stake other than selecting the fastest route to the highway. For example, perhaps proving the other friend wrong is of some serious importance, or acquiescing, or deferring to avoid a conflict in the relationship. Consider a different case where I am having a disagreement with a friend over whether or not dogs make good house pets. I might defer to her belief that they do not make good house pets because I know that she is afraid of dogs and arguing with her over such a trivial matter (for me) would needlessly upset her. I might also be interested in being a *sympathetic friend* by adopting a belief that she holds. Assuming that we both provided two distinct evidential scenarios, e.g., cases where dogs bite and make horrible house pets and cases where dogs show wanted affection and help reduce daily stress, the change in my belief about dogs may still fail to result from either rational consensus or from evaluating and accepting my friend's evidence about dogs. Instead, my belief change was the result of my deference to a friend and for the benefit of that relationship. Some might argue that my belief change may not to be sincere as it does not represent what I truly believe about dogs as house pets. That is, the reason for my belief change seem *affective* and non-epistemic and thus unlikely to constitute a real belief change. However, I would argue that it is equally plausible for belief change via disagreement to stem from reasons that are not directly related to the evidence at hand. Similar to how our negative perceptions of others may unwittingly lead us to deflate credibility in testimonial scenarios, our positive perceptions of others may lead us to extend undue credibility to poor evidence in cases of disagreement.

It may also be the case that improvements to the truth-related imperfections of our beliefs via disagreement can get stymied by what knowers take as evidence in the first place. Although epistemic peers may engage in disagreement, even involving the same evidential scenario, there is no reason to think that they will come to the same conclusion about either the evidence or the need for belief revision. There may be cases where epistemic stalemate occurs because neither party agrees to the other's interpretation of the same evidence *and* neither party consents to a method or principle to resolve that stalemate, e.g., the *Principle of Indifference*. This situation is further complicated in cases where knowers are not considered to be epistemic peers, but, due to unjust credibility deflations or inflations, they judge each other (or themselves) to be either epistemic superiors or inferiors. In theoretically ideal cases, epistemic superiority describes cases where the epistemically superior knower has (a) evidence or expertise unavailable to the epistemically inferior knower, or (b) analytical or evaluative skills that the epistemically inferior knower does not possess. In these cases, there are good reasons for the epistemically inferior knower to be less confident in their own beliefs about a given *p* or even to revise their beliefs in light of the epistemically superior knower's evidence. That is, there is something about disagreement with an epistemic superior that should make an epistemic inferior *less confident* in their own beliefs regardless of whether or not they ultimately readjust or revise those beliefs.

What is not clear, however, is that we ought to give more weight to an epistemic superior's beliefs without saying something substantive about the quality of the evidence or quality of the capacity for expertise. For example, there is no "view from nowhere" from which we can say anything conclusive about the *evidential content* of an epistemic superior's beliefs without evaluating the evidence or the capacities of the epistemic superior for ourselves. Notice how this complicates assignments of epistemic superiority and epistemic inferiority by introducing second-order subjectivity. It is from this second-order subjectivity that issues of prejudice can arise. For how can we make evaluations of epistemic superiority and inferiority when our negative perceptions of others make extensions of credibility so loaded in the first place? From the perspective of epistemic injustice, as with other forms of testimonial exchange, epistemic disagreement will also be impacted by asymmetrical social power. The negatively prejudicial stereotypes that deflate marginalized speaker's credibility will mark those speakers as epistemically inferior before assessment of evidence or reliability can be made. This taints the possibility of just disagreement between epistemic superiors and inferiors. Systematic testimonial injustice may also fully *preclude* the possibility of peer disagreement as marginalized knowers will rarely, if ever, be perceived as epistemic peers. Epistemic labor may help facilitate better disagreements as marginalized knowers employ non-epistemic strategies to gain credibility in the eyes of dominant knowers, however, this merely doubles down on epistemic injustice, further excluding marginalized knowers from real epistemic peerhood.

Implicit bias and negative stereotypes may complicate even the most well-intentioned epistemic goals of dominant knowers if they still subconsciously think of marginalized knowers as epistemically inferior. As such, disagreement is implicated as a failed mechanism by which dominant knowers come to revise their beliefs about marginalized knowers and marginalized epistemic resources. Instead some other forms of epistemic intervention will need to be considered in order to mitigate persistent testimonial injustice and the need for epistemic labor. To clarify, it is not clear that dominant knowers can fail to encode negative stereotypes (as *all* knowers encode negative stereotypes) and thus disagreement, like other testimonial exchanges, will be unjustly influenced by the negative stereotypes held by those with both social power and identity power. Thus, disagreement, even in moderately successful cases, will not offer a consistent mechanism by which dominant knowers can engage in non-prejudicial discussions with marginalized knowers about the potential for collective epistemic resources. It seems first that our epistemic interventions will have to contend with the nonconscious psychological dispositions that corrupt disagreement. As with general cases of testimony, it seems unclear that dominant knowers will consider concerns of evidence and truth as so compelling that they can, or will attempt to, circumvent those biases in the name of less prejudicial testimonial exchanges. In cases of disagreement, however, dominant knowers *might* consider disagreement as compelling enough grounds to attempt mitigating bias but I leave that as an open issue. The question is: if such grounds *are* found to be compelling, then is it even possible to dominant knowers to do so? (This will almost assuredly exclude dominant knowers who hold *explicit* biases and prejudices as they will be much more resistant to desire for fruitful disagreement.)

Miranda Fricker has argued that self-regulation of implicit bias is possible, citing the work of social psychologist, Margo Monteith. She argues that knowers can be brought to self-regulate using "alertness to cues for control" primarily backed by negative self-directed feelings like guilt or shame (Fricker 2010, 165). The hope seems to be in "catching oneself" in the midst of negative identity prejudicial perceptions and adjusting accordingly. Although Fricker is not wedded exclusively to these conscious practices, she *is* wedded to epistemic practices rooted in dominant knowers' having relevant motivations to achieve some end, which seems, on the face of things, to move in the same direction that I go here. Her Aristotelian model moves from motivation to habituation such that remediation process moves from conscious and motivated prescription to nonconscious and reflexive behavior: "The broadly Aristotelian model I've adopted in the book is motive-based; but motive-based virtue incorporates a reliability condition (reliability in achieving the end of one's good motive) and there is no reason why this reliability should not be achieved by way of sheer habit or other sub-personal mechanism" (Fricker 2010, 166). However, before motive-based virtues can be habituated, they must be consciously and consistently acted upon in relevant circumstances. Habituation is the end-state of conscious practice—but how can this occur if knowers are unaware of their nonconscious biases in the first place? Notice that we are back to the same problem found in chapter 1.

Following Fricker, Jennifer Saul agrees that conscious self-regulation of implicit bias is possible, citing studies by Jack Glaser and Eric D. Knowles, Gordon B. Moskowitz and Peizhong Li, Saaid A. Mendoza et al., Irene V. Blair et al., and Kerry Kawakami et al. According to Saul, these studies strongly suggest that self-regulation "done the right way" offers a successful mechanism by which we can mitigate negative stereotypes and implicit bias (2017, 465). What is not clear is that these mechanisms are or can be as successful as

Fricker and Saul claim or that conscious interventions into implicit bias will solve the problem of disagreement. How well do these conscious strategies and interventions really work and what exactly are we entitled to extrapolate from them? More than that, as asked by Jeanine Weekes Schroer (2015) and Lacey Davidson (2019), do we have reason to assume the epistemic superiority of social scientific research on implicit bias over the phenomenological reporting of marginalized knowers? That is, can implicit bias data tell us all that we need to know about, say, racism or sexism? Lastly, and perhaps most importantly, what is the real-world applicability of these study results? I think it unlikely that either social psychologists or philosophers have found the silver bullet for remedying implicit bias and negative stereotypes at their source. We would need to know much more than we currently do about our neurobiological socialization to particular patterns of bias and prejudice in order to get there. However, such proclamations might be premature without looking first to the studies at issue.

In the following section, I offer an overview of some of the studies mentioned by Fricker and Saul. This is not intended to be an exhaustive look at a large body social psychological literature. Instead it is intended to cast a bit of doubt on how these intervention models are used by philosophers to suggest that the way out of implicit bias is in the adoption of conscious strategies that yield real-world results. It is intended to cast doubt on the idea that racist, sexist, homophobic, and transphobic discrimination is merely a training session or reflective exercise away. This type of thinking devalues the experiences of marginalized bodies who *live* through racism, sexism, homophobia, transphobia, and ableism by implying that they are, at least at the level of individuals, merely "thinking gone wrong." This minimizes how pervasive such social experiences are and the myriad ways in which their effects of seep into marrow of the bodies and psyches of marginalized knowers. Worse still, they imply that marginalized knowers who claim that our experiences are not understood and that our testimonies are found noncredible are not giving the right type of evidence, i.e., *scientific* evidence, or even giving evidence that matters. As Weekes Schroer argues:

> Research [has] become entangled in a corrupted system of knowledge that produces semi-truths while disguising its own corruption. Specifically, what superficially appears to be a neutral lens of analysis by which the discourse on racism can be improved—increasing the credibility of testimony about the hurts of racism by translating it into data on the harms of racism—actually serves to disguise and further entrench the idea that the people of colors' first-person accounts of the hurts and harms of racism are not credible. (2015, 5)

In order to untangle some of the implicit bias research, both methodologically and in terms of real-world applicability, I break up the studies offered
by Saul into four intuitive model types: strategy models, discrepancy models, IAT models, and egalitarian goal models. I start with Kawakami et al.
and Mendoza et al. as examples of *strategy models* before moving on to
discrepancy models, IAT models, and so on. Some minor details have been
omitted for the sake of clarity but I hope that I have made overall methodologies and conclusions clear enough without suffering from excessive
oversimplification.

Kawakami et al. use Devine and Monteith's conception of a (negative)
stereotype as being similar to a "bad habit" that a knower needs to "kick";
their experiment models strategies that can be employed to aid in the kicking
of the habit of stereotype activation, or the "increased cognitive accessibility
of characteristics associated with a particular group" (Kawakami et al. 2005,
68–69).[1] In a previous study, Kawakami et al. asked research participants
presented with photographs of black individuals and white individuals with
stereotypical traits and non-stereotypical traits listed under each photograph
to respond "No" to stereotypical traits and "Yes" to non-stereotypical traits
(Kawakami et al. 2005, 69).[2] The study found that "participants who were
extensively trained to negate racial stereotypes initially also demonstrated
stereotype activation, this effect was eliminated by the extensive training.
Furthermore, Kawakami et al. found that practice effects of this type lasted up
to 24 h following the training" (2005, 69). Kawakami et al. used this training
to ground an experiment aimed at strategies for reducing stereotype activation in the preference for men over women in leadership for managerial positions. Despite the training, they found that there was "no difference between
Nonstereotypic Association Training and No Training conditions . . . participants were indeed attempting to choose the best candidate overall, in these
conditions *there was an overall pattern of discrimination against women
relative to men* in recommended hiring for a managerial position (Glick,
1991; Rudman & Glick, 1999)" (Kawakami et al. 2005, 73, my italics) .

Substantive conclusions are difficult to make by a single study but one
critical point of note is how learning occurred in the training but improved
stereotype activation did not. What, exactly, are we to make of this result?
Kawakami et al. claim that "similar levels of bias in both the Training and
No Training conditions implicates the influence of correction processes that
limit the effectiveness of training" (2005, 73). That is, they attribute the lack
of influence of corrective processes on a variety of contributing factors that
limited the effectiveness of the strategy. Notice, however, that this does not
implicate the strategy itself. Most notably Kawakami et al. found that "when
people have the time and opportunity to control their responses [they] may
be strongly shaped by personal values and temporary motivations, strategies

aimed at changing the automatic activation of stereotypes will not [necessarily] result in reduced discrimination" (2005, 74). This suggests that although the strategies failed to reduce stereotype activation they may still be helpful in limited circumstances "when impressions are more deliberative" (2005, 74). One wonders under what conditions such impressions *can* be more deliberative? More than that, how useful are such limited-condition strategies for dealing with everyday life and every day automatic stereotype activation?

Mendoza et al. tested the effectiveness of "implementation intentions" as a strategy to reduce the activation or expression of implicit stereotypes using the Shooter Task.[3] They tested both "distraction-inhibiting" implementation intentions and "response-facilitating" implementation intentions. Distraction-inhibiting intentions are strategies "designed to engage inhibitory control," such as inhibiting the perception of distracting or biasing information, while "response-facilitating" intentions are strategies designed to enhance goal attainment by focusing on specific goal-directed actions (Mendoza et al. 2010, 513–514). In the first study, Mendoza et al. asked participants to repeat the on-screen phrase, *"If I see a person, then I will ignore his race!"* in their heads and then type the phrase into the computer. The result was that study participants had a reduced number of errors in the Shooter Task. But let's come back to if and how we might be able to usefully extrapolate from these results. The second study compared a simple-goal strategy with an implementation intention strategy. Study participants in the simple-goal strategy group were asked to follow the strategy, "I will always shoot a person I see with a gun!" and "I will never shoot a person I see with an object!" Study participants in the implementation intention strategy group were asked to use a conditional, if-then, strategy instead: "If I see a person with an object, then I will not shoot!" Mendoza et al. found that a response-facilitating implementation intention "enhanced controlled processing but did not affect automatic stereotyping processing," while a distraction-inhibiting implementation intention "was associated with an increase in controlled processing and a decrease in automatic stereotyping processes" (2010, 520).

Note that if the goal is to reduce automatic stereotype activation through reflexive control that only a distraction-inhibiting strategy achieved the desired goal. Note also how the successful use of a distraction-inhibiting strategy may require a type of "non-messy" social environment unachievable outside of a laboratory experiment.[4] Or, as Mendoza et al. rightly note: "The current findings suggest that the quick interventions typically used in psychological experiments may be more effective in modulating behavioral responses or the temporary accessibility of stereotypes than in undoing highly edified knowledge structures" (2010, 520). The hope, of course, is that distraction-inhibiting strategies can help dominant knowers reduce automatic stereotype activation and response-facilitated strategies can help dominant knowers internalize controlled processing such that negative bias and stereotyping can be (one day) reflexively controlled as well. But these are only hopes. The only thing that we can rightly conclude from these results is that if we ask a dominant knower to focus on an internal command, they will do so. The result is that the activation of negative bias fails to occur. This *does not* mean that the knower has reduced their internalized negative biases and prejudices *or* that they can continue to act on the internal commands in the future (in fact, subsequent studies reveal the effects are short-lived).[5] As Mendoza et al. also note: "In psychometric terms, these strategies are designed to enhance accuracy without necessarily affecting bias. That is, a person may still have a tendency to associate Black people with violence and thus be more likely to shoot unarmed Blacks than to shoot unarmed Whites" (2010, 520). Despite hope for these strategies, there is very little to support their real-world applicability.

I would extend a similar critique to Margot Monteith's *discrepancy model*. Monteith's often cited study uses two experiments to investigate prejudice-related discrepancies in the behaviors of low-prejudice (LP) and high-prejudice (HP) individuals and the ability to engage in self-regulated prejudice reduction. In the first experiment, LP and HP heterosexual study participants were asked to evaluate two law school applications, one for an implied gay applicant and one for an implied heterosexual applicant. Study participants "were led to believe that they had evaluated a gay law school applicant negatively because of his sexual orientation"; they were tricked into a "discrepancy-activated condition" or a condition that was at odds with their believed prejudicial state (Monteith 1993, 472). All of the study participants were then told that the applications were identical and that those who had rejected the gay applicant had done so because of the applicant's sexual orientation. It is important to note that the applicants qualifications were not, in fact, identical. The gay applicant's application materials were made to look worse than the heterosexual applicant's materials. This was done to compel the rejection of the applicant. Study participants were then provided a follow-up questionnaire and essay allegedly written by a professor who wanted to know (a) "why people often have difficulty avoiding negative responses toward gay men," and (b) "how people can eliminate their negative responses toward gay men" (Monteith 1993, 474). Researchers asked study participants to record their reactions to the faculty essay and write down as much they could remember about what they read in the essay. The study participants were then told about the deception in the experiment and told why such deception was incorporated in the study.

Monteith found that "low and high prejudiced subjects alike experienced discomfort after violating their personal standards for responding to a gay man, but only low prejudiced subjects experienced negative self-directed affect" (1993, 475). Low prejudiced, LP, "discrepancy-activated subjects," also spent more time reading the faculty essay and "showed superior recall for the portion of the essay concerning why prejudice-related discrepancies arise" (Monteith 1993, 477). The "discrepancy experience" generated negative self-directed affect, or *guilt*, for LP study participants with the hope that the guilt would (a) "motivate discrepancy reduction (e.g., Rokeach, 1973)" and (b) "serve to establish strong cues for punishment (cf. Gray, 1982)" (Monteith 1993, 477). The hope is that the experiment results point to the existence of a self-regulatory mechanism that can replace automatic stereotype activation with "belief-based responses"; however, "it is important to note that the initiation of self-regulatory mechanisms is dependent on recognizing and interpreting one's responses as discrepant from one's personal beliefs (Monteith 1993, 477). The discrepancy between what one is shown to believe and what one professes to believe (whether real or manufactured, as in the experiment) is aimed at getting dominant knowers to engage in heightened self-focus due to negative self-directed affect. The operating idea of Monteith's study is that self-directed affect would lead to a kind of corrective belief-making process that is both less prejudicial and future-directed.

But if it's *guilt* that's doing the psychological work in these cases, then it's not clear that dominant knowers would not find other means to ease such feelings. Why wouldn't it be the case that generating negative self-directed affect would point a knower toward anything they deem necessary to restore a more positive sense of self? To this, Monteith makes the following concession:

> Steele (1988; Steele & Liu, 1983) contended that restoration of one's self-image after a discrepancy experience may not entail discrepancy reduction if other opportunities for self-affirmation are available. For example, Steele (1988) suggested that a smoker who wants to quit might spend more time with his or her children to resolve the threat to the self-concept engendered by the psychological inconsistency created by smoking. Similarly, Tesser and Cornell (1991) found that different behaviors appeared to feed into a general "self-evaluation reservoir." *It follows that prejudice-related discrepancy experiences may not facilitate the self-regulation of prejudiced responses if other means to restoring one's self-regard are available.* (1993, 482, my italics)

Additionally, she notes that even if individuals are committed to the reducing or "unlearning" automatic stereotyping, they "may become frustrated and disengage from the self-regulatory cycle, abandoning their goal to eliminate prejudice-like responses" (Monteith 1993, 483). Tamar Szabó Gendler also suggests that cognitive exhaustion, or cognitive depletion, can occurs after intergroup exchanges as well. Consistent intergroup activity may make "unlearning" cognitively costly due to burnout or exhaustion. This may make it even less likely that a dominant knower will continue to feel guilty and use that guilt to inhibit the activation of negative stereotypes when they find themselves struggling with cognitive depletion.

The last two models are Glaser and Knowles' and Blair et al.'s *Implicit Association Test (IAT) models* and Moskowitz and Li's *egalitarian goal model*. Like Mendoza et al.'s implementation intentions, Glaser and Knowles measure implicit mechanisms to inhibit automatic stereotype activation, or implicit motivations to control prejudice (IMCP), in terms of implicit negative attitudes toward prejudice, or NAP, and implicit beliefs that oneself is prejudiced, or BOP. This is done by retooling the IAT to fit both NAP and BOP: "To measure NAP we constructed an Implicit Association Test (IAT) that pairs the categories 'prejudice' and 'tolerance' with the categories 'bad' and 'good.' BOP was assessed with an Implicit Association Test (IAT) pairing 'prejudiced' and 'tolerant' with 'me' and 'not me'" (Glaser and Knowles 2008, 165). Study participants were then administered the Shooter Task, the IMCP measures, and the Race Prejudice (Implicit Association Test [IAT]) and Race-Weapons Stereotype (RWS) tests in a fixed order. Glaser and Knowles predicted that IMCP as an implicit goal for those *high* in IMCP "should be able to short-circuit the effect of implicit anti-Black stereotypes on automatic anti-Black behavior" (2008, 167). The results seemed to suggest this was the case. Glaser and Knowles found that study participants who viewed prejudiced as particularly bad "[showed] no relationship between implicit stereotypes and spontaneous behavior" (2008, 170).

There are a few considerations missing from the evaluation of the study results. First, with regard to the Shooter Task, Glaser and Knowles found that "the interaction of target race by object type, reflecting the Shooter Bias, was not statistically significant" (2008, 168). That is, the strength of the relationship that Correll et al. found between study participants and the (high) likelihood that they would "shoot" at black targets was not found in the study. Additionally, they note that they "eliminated time pressure" from the task itself. Although it was not suggested that this impacted the usefulness of the measure of shooter bias, it is difficult to imagine that it did not do so. To this, they footnote the following caveats:

> Variance in the degree and direction of the stereotype endorsement points to one reason for our failure to replicate Correll et al.'s (2002) typically robust Shooter Bias effect. That is, our sample appears to have held stereotypes linking Blacks and weapons/aggression/danger to a lesser extent than did Correll and colleagues' participants. In Correll et al. (2002, 2003), participants one *SD* below the mean on the stereotype measure reported an anti-Black stereotype, whereas similarly low scorers on our RWS Implicit Association Test (IAT) evidenced a stronger association between *Whites* and weapons. Further, the adaptation of

the Shooter Task reported here may have been less sensitive than the procedure developed by Correll and colleagues. In the service of shortening and simplifying the task, we used fewer trials, eliminated time pressure and rewards for speed and accuracy, and presented only one background per trial. (Glaser and Knowles 2008, 168)

Glaser and Knowles note that the interaction of the RWS with the Shooter Task results proved "significant," however, if the Shooter Bias failed to materialize (in the standard Correll et al. way) with study participants, it is difficult to see how the RWS was measuring anything except itself, generally speaking. This is further complicated by the fact that the interaction between the Shooter Bias and the RWS revealed "a mild reverse stereotype associating Whites with weapons ($d = -0.15$) and a strong stereotype associating Blacks with weapons ($d = 0.83$), respectively" (Glaser and Knowles 2008, 169).

Recall that Glaser and Knowles aimed to show that participants high in IMCP would be able to inhibit implicit anti-Black stereotypes and thus inhibit automatic anti-Black behaviors. Using NAP and BOP as proxies for implicit control, participants high in NAP and moderate in BOP—as those with moderate BOP will be motivated to avoid bias—should show the weakest association between RWS and Shooter Bias. Instead, the lowest levels of Shooter Bias were seen in "low NAP, high BOP, and low RWS" study participants, or those who do not disapprove of prejudice, would describe themselves as prejudiced, and also showed lowest levels of RWS (Glaser and Knowles 2008, 169).[6] They note that neither "NAP nor BOP alone was significantly related to the Shooter Bias," but "the influence of RWS on Shooter Bias remained significant" (Glaser and Knowles 2008, 169). In fact, greater bias was actually found with higher NAP and BOP levels. This bias seems to map on to the initial results of the Shooter Task results. It is most likely that RWS was the most important measure in this study for assessing implicit bias, not, as the study claims, for assessing implicit motivation to control prejudice. It is also not clear that the RWS is not capturing *explicit bias* instead of implicit bias in this study. At the point at which study participants were tasked with the RWS, automatic stereotype activation may have been inhibited just by virtue of study participants involvement in the Shooter Task and IAT assessments regarding race-related prejudice. That is, *race-sensitivity* was brought to consciousness in the sequencing of the test process.

Although we cannot get into the heads of the study participants, this counter explanation seems a compelling possibility. That is, that the sequential tasks involved in the study captured study participants' ability to increase focus and increase conscious attention to the race-related IAT test. Additionally, it is possible that some study participants can both cue and follow their own conscious internal commands, "If I see a black face, I won't judge!" Consider that this is exactly how implementation intentions work. Consider that this is also how Armageddon chess and other speed strategy games work. In Park et al.'s follow-up study on IMCP and cognitive depletion, they retreat somewhat from their initial claims about the implicit nature of IMCP:

> We cannot state for certain that our measure of IMCP reflects a purely non-conscious construct, nor that differential speed to "shoot" Black armed men vs. White armed men in a computer simulation reflects purely automatic processes. Most likely, the underlying stereotypes, goals, and behavioral responses represent a blend of conscious and nonconscious influences . . . Based on the results of the present study and those of Glaser and Knowles (2008), it would be premature to conclude that IMCP is a purely and wholly automatic construct . . . it is not yet clear whether high IMCP participants initiate control of prejudice without intention; whether implicit control of prejudice can itself be inhibited, if for some reason someone wanted to; nor whether IMCP-instigated control of spontaneous bias occurs without awareness. (Park et al. 2008, 416)

If the IMCP potentially measures low-level conscious attention, this makes the question of what implicit measurements *actually* measure in the context of sequential tasks all the more important. In the two final examples, Blair et al.'s study on the use of counter-stereotype imagery using the IAT and Moskowitz and Li's study on the use of counter-stereotype egalitarian goals, we are again confronted with the issue of sequencing. In the study by Moskowitz and Li, study participants were asked to write down an example of a time when "they failed to live up to the ideal specified by an egalitarian goal, and to do so by relaying an event relating to African American men" (Moskowitz and Peizhong 2011, 106). They were then given a series of computerized lexicon decision tasks (LDTs), primes involving photographs of Black and white faces, and stereotypical and non-stereotypical attributes of Black people, e.g., criminal, lazy, stupid, nervous, indifferent, nosy. Over a series of four experiments, Moskowitz and Li found that when egalitarian goals were "accessible," study participants were able to successfully generate stereotype inhibition. Blair et al. asked study participants to use counter-stereotypical (CS) gender imagery over a series of five experiments, e.g., "Think of a strong, capable woman," and then administered a series of implicit measures, including the Implicit Association Test (IAT).

Similar to Moskowitz and Li, they found that CS gender imagery was successful in reducing implicit gender stereotypes leaving "little doubt that the CS mental imagery per se was responsible for diminishing implicit stereotypes" (Blair et al. 2001, 837). In both cases, the study participants were explicitly called upon to focus their attention on experiences and imagery pertaining to negative stereotypes before the implicit measures, i.e., tasks, were administered. Again it is not clear that the implicit measures measured the supposed target. In the case of Moskowitz and Li's experiment, the study participants began by relating moments in their lives where they failed to live up to their goals. However, those goals can only be understood within a particular social and political framework where holding negatively prejudicial beliefs about African-American men is often *explicitly* judged harshly, even if not implicitly so. Given this, we might assume that the study participants were compelled into a negative affective state. But does this matter? As suggested by the study by Monteith, and later study by Amodio et al., guilt can be a powerful tool (Amodio et al. 2007, 524–530).

If guilt was produced during the early stages of the experiment, it may have also participated in the inhibition of stereotype activation. Moskowitz and Li note that "during targeted questioning in the debriefing, no participants expressed any conscious intent to inhibit stereotypes on the task, nor saw any of the tasks performed during the computerized portion of the experiment as related to the egalitarian goals they had undermined earlier in the session" (2011, 108). But guilt does not have to be conscious for it to produce effects. The guilt produced by recalling a moment of negative bias could be part and parcel of a larger feeling of moral failure. Moskowitz and Li need to disambiguate potentially competing implicit motivations for stereotype inhibition. This, I think, is a limitation of the study. However, the same case could be made for CS imagery. Blair et al. note that it is, in fact, possible that they too have missed competing motivations and competing explanations for stereotype inhibition. Particularly, they suggest that by emphasizing counter-stereotyping the researchers "may have communicated the importance of avoiding stereotypes and increased their motivation to do so" (Blair et al. 2001, 838). Still, the researchers dismiss that this would lead to better (faster, more accurate) performance of the Implicit Association Test (IAT), but that is merely asserting that the IAT *must* measure exactly what the IAT claims it does. Fast, accurate, and conscious measures are excluded from that claim. Complicated internal motivations are excluded from that claim. But on what grounds? Consider Klaus Fielder et al.'s argument that the IAT is susceptible to faking and strategic processing, or C. Miguel Brendl et al.'s argument that it is not possible to infer a single cause from IAT results, or Russell H. Fazio and Michael A. Olson's claim "the Implicit Association Test (IAT) has little to do with what is automatically activated in response to a given stimulus."[7]

These studies call into question the claim that implicit measures like the IAT can measure implicit bias in the clear, problem-free manner that is often suggested in the literature. Implicit interventions in implicit bias that utilize the IAT are difficult to support for this reason. Implicit interventions that utilize sequential tasks are difficult to support for a similar reason as well. Of course, this is also live debate—and the problems I discuss here are far from the only ones that plague this type of research.[8] That said, when it comes to this research we are too often left wondering if the measure itself is measuring the right thing. Are we capturing implicit bias or some other socially generated phenomenon? Are the measured changes we see in study results reflecting the validity of the instrument or the cognitive maneuverings of study participants? These are all critical questions that need sussing out. The temporary result is that the target conclusion that implicit interventions will lead to reductions in real-world discrimination will move further away.[9] We find evidence of this conclusion in Forscher et al.'s meta-analysis of 492 implicit interventions:

> We found little evidence that changes in implicit measures translated into changes in explicit measures and behavior, and we observed limitations in the evidence base for implicit malleability and change. These results produce a challenge for practitioners who seek to address problems that are presumed to be caused by automatically retrieved associations, as there was little evidence showing that change in implicit measures will result in changes for explicit measures or behavior . . . Our results suggest that current interventions that attempt to change implicit measures will not consistently change behavior in these domains. These results also produce a challenge for researchers who seek to understand the nature of human cognition because they raise new questions about the causal role of automatically retrieved associations . . . To better understand what the results mean, future research should innovate with more reliable and valid implicit, explicit, and behavioral tasks, intensive manipulations, longitudinal measurement of outcomes, heterogeneous samples, and diverse topics of study. (2018)

Implicit bias is related to the culture one is in and the stereotypes it produces, thus, instead of insisting on changing individuals in order to reduce bias and stereotyping, what if we insisted on changing our social spaces and social institutions? As Linda Martín Alcoff notes: "We must be willing to explore more mechanisms for redress, such as extensive educational reform, more serious projects of affirmative action, and curricular mandates that would help to correct the identity prejudices built up out of faulty narratives of history" (2010, 132). I come back to this claim in chapter 5. At the heart of the question, however, is a suggestion that evaluations of interventions of implicit bias alone are unlikely to solve the social problems that implicit bias has and is creating. Social science will not give us a clear way out of racism, sexism, gender discrimination, etc., at the moment, it may only give us tools for seeing ourselves a bit more clearly. Taking the study results further than this may only be another form of willful ignorance, an active refusal to acknowledge the limitations of dominant forms of knowing, while omitting or erasing other marginalized forms of knowing. It reinforces the belief that science can cure all social and epistemic ills while never taking full stock of the systems that create those ills, and in its wake, we are left with a series of half-baked solutions masquerading as serious remedies.

But how ought we think about epistemic responsibility and epistemic remediation for testimonial injustice and epistemic labor if disagreement is tainted and first-order interventions into implicit bias and negative stereotyping are not possible? Here I suggest that we look to real-world attempts to achieve collective meaning-making, cases where the role of implicit bias and negative stereotyping are made explicit as impediments to collective knowing, and willful ignorance is addressed by way of sympathetic dominant knowers' amplification of marginalized epistemic resources. For example, in targeted educational environments, such as in African and African American studies programs, or during political/policy change campaigns, such as Stacey Abrams' Fair Fight campaign organizing against marginalized voter suppression in Georgia and Texas. I refer to these epistemic spaces as "evolving epistemic frameworks" because of their emphasis on dominant knowers and marginalized knowers amplifying marginalized epistemic resources, e.g., voter disenfranchisement versus *voter fraud*, within the dominant epistemic framework. In evolving epistemic frameworks, willful ignorance, negative stereotyping, and the implicit and explicit biases of dominant knowers are highlighted as critical factors to explore in order to achieve the collective goals of the evolving framework.

I use the term "sympathetic dominant knower" above to describe dominant knowers with sincere and significant interests in epistemic spaces dedicated to marginalized knowing and marginalized epistemic resources. The exclusion of marginalized epistemic resources from the dominant epistemic framework serves an important motivating factor for sympathetic dominant knowers' engagement with the evolving framework alongside a vested interest in the amplification of marginalized epistemic resources. I take the student-led political organization created in the aftermath of the Parkland school shooting as a core example of an evolving epistemic framework. The organization, established by survivors of the shooting, initiated a public campaign to end gun violence quickly after the event. They organized large-scale public demonstrations and nationwide events, including the March for Our Lives and the National School Walkout Day, and went on to form a political action committee, Never Again MSD, named after Marjory Stoneman Douglas high school where the shooting took place. Leveraging social media platforms like Twitter and Facebook, the organization was able to engage the mainstream media and the public-at-large in die-ins, rallies, voter registration events, and televised debates with pro-gun politicians, in order to advocate for sensible gun reform legislation. The hashtags, #NeverAgain and #EnoughIsEnough, marked both the movement and its founders across a variety of social media spaces and led corporations like Hertz, MetLife, Delta Airlines, and United Airlines to sever ties with the National Rifle Association and those who profited from National Rifle Association membership.

At the same time, from communities of color, another narrative emerged about the Never Again movement. Activists of color noted, with some frustration, that the mainstream media treated white survivors of gun violence with greater concern than it treated Black and Hispanic survivors of gun violence (Green 2018).[10] Noting the discrepancy in coverage, Black Lives Matter activists argued that the outpouring of emotional and financial support for the Never Again movement was at odds with the way that politicians and the mainstream media treated Black activists fighting for the same reforms. Black activists were called "thugs" and "extremists" for advocating for gun reform while white activists were publicly praised as "inspiring" and "a powerful force," with comparisons made to 1960s Freedom Riders (Lockhart 2018). Black Lives Matter co-founder, Patrisse Cullors, noted:

> White people get to be everything. They get to victims, they get to be heroes. And black people, unfortunately, continue to be criminalized for our moments of courage, for our moments of mourning and grieving . . . when we go out into the streets, when we protest, when we demand for our lives to matter, we're given heavy police repression. Why don't black people get to be victims? That's the question we have to ask ourselves. (Lockhart 2018)

We can frame this as an issue of willful ignorance, one where dominant knowers refused to employ the epistemic resources of marginalized knowers and thus refused to recognize the similarities between white survivors of gun violence and Black survivors of gun violence. The result being that white survivors were understood as *victims* of violent and unjust social experiences and Black survivors were understood as *thugs* who were, in some important sense, responsible for bringing violent social experiences upon themselves. However, this is also a case of an evolving epistemic framework or an epistemic space where (some) sympathetic dominant knowers' biases and prejudices are made explicit in order to engage in meaningful discussions about collective ends, i.e., ending gun violence, while using marginalized epistemic resources. By reaching out to activists of color and ceding public space to organizations of color, like Chicago-based Peace Warriors, the organizers behind Never Again attempted to address their willful ignorance and amplify marginalized testimonies and marginalized epistemic resources. Like testimonial virtue, amplification is a form of *extending* or inflating the credibility of marginalized knowers and is achieved primarily by having the relevant social power. This illustrates both the power asymmetry inherent to evolving epistemic frameworks and the ways in which they are predicated on background relations of social power characteristic of dominant knowing. Consider the following statement made by Emma González of Never Again:

> Those who face gun violence on a level that we have only just glimpsed from our gated communities have never had their voices heard in their entire lives the way that we have in these few weeks alone . . . Since we all share in feeling this pain and know all too well how it feels to have to grow up at the snap of a finger, we were able to cover a lot of ground in communicating our experiences . . . People of color in inner-cities and everywhere have been dealing with this for a despicably long time, and the media cycles just don't cover the violence the way they did here. The platform us Parkland [students] have established is to be shared with every person, black or white, gay or straight, religious or not, who has experienced gun violence. (Brown-Dean 2019, 222)

The organizers of Never Again tried to acknowledge their own social and epistemic privilege, realizing that they could use their social power to both confer credibility and to turn the lens of dominant knowing toward marginalized testimonies and resources, e.g., through appeals to the mainstream media. In doing so, the organizers of Never Again also came to see how their own dominant epistemic resources, and their own dominant ways of meaning-making, were limited by how they were socially situated and thus not representative of the entire epistemic terrain. This is an important step in addressing willful ignorance as it reveals, at minimum, that there are epistemic resources to consider beyond dominant resources. Although it may be the case that they never come to know beyond their own social location (as resolving willful ignorance does take work), they can see how their dominant social location distorts the wider landscape of knowledge-production and meaning-making. We should ask, of course, is that enough?

In the context of evolving epistemic frameworks, sympathetic dominant knowers may also come to see themselves as *allies* of marginalized knowers, although they *need not* self-identify as allies as a precondition to participation in an evolving framework. However, as discussed in Chapter 2, there can be problems with declarations of allyship. As Rachel McKinnon argues, allies can behave in ways that explicitly or implicitly challenge marginalized speakers' assertions despite their claims of providing "safe spaces" to speak and extensions of epistemic credibility. This can happen if an ally doubts or fails to believe a marginalized speaker's testimony about their own oppression despite the fact that the marginalized speaker is in a better position to know. Recall that McKinnon refers to this as a form of *gaslighting*. Marginalized speakers are often vulnerable in relationships with dominant allies because we are lead to believe that they will not engage in unjust credibility deficits. Instead, because of the nature of the social relationship, allyship suggests an *inflation* of epistemic credibility about our experiences within marginalized social locations. Thus failures of allyship can also put an implicit demand on marginalized speakers to engage in epistemic labor when we do not expect to do so. Dominant allies may change the nature of the social and epistemic relationship by informally rescinding extensions of credibility in the form of epistemic gaslighting (e.g., "Are you *sure* that's the way it really happened? Mark wouldn't tell racist jokes like that."). Unjust credibility deficits in the form of gaslighting illustrate just how easily trust can breakdown within evolving frameworks. This is because, ultimately, evolving frameworks still sit within the dominant epistemic framework, and dominant knowers can easily call upon the epistemic authority conferred to them by that framework.

The credibility of marginalized speakers in evolving frameworks is always precarious due to social and identity power asymmetry. Assignments of credibility are based on the choices made by sympathetic dominant knowers to extend credibility to marginalized knowing not, as one might think, on the credibility of the assertions themselves. Extensions of credibility are not predicated on sympathetic dominant knowers being about to "hear well" or "know well." In fact, the temporary ceding of social and epistemic power often occurs despite the fact that sympathetic dominant knowers fail to understand the claims made by marginalized knowers. (This may be part of what goes wrong in the cases McKinnon describes as "allies behaving badly.") Consider that even in the case of Never Again, the organizers consistently invoked the language of "we" and "us" as different from "them" despite the alleged collectivity of the endeavor. Their language reinforced the focus on white survivors of gun violence by picking out "we" and "us" as referential stand-in for *whiteness* despite the fact that the term could, or should, be referentially ambiguous. In González's speech, "we" picks out "survivors" but it also picks out racialized and class-based identities as well, e.g., those in "gated communities" versus those in "inner-cities." Whiteness is so naturally presumed over other types of *otherness*, e.g., Blackness, that what is presumed to be natural becomes *naturalized*. When reading the speech above it is easy to overlook how "we" and "us" are framed against "their" and "people of color" and how that "we" subtly erases the students of color and people of color *within* the Parkland community itself. In this particular example, although well-intentioned, the implicit framing of *whiteness* against *otherness* also picks out those victims or survivors worthy of public sympathy and those who fail to be worthy of public sympathy. I highlight this not to discount their good motivations but to illustrate how easy it is for language to reify the social concepts and social power relations of the dominant framework.

I also highlight this example in order to illustrate how, like testimonial virtue, sympathetic dominant knowers *extending* epistemic credibility to marginalized knowers is a remedy without long-term design. This is because extensions of epistemic credibility do little to dismantle the dominant frameworks that confer and *deny* epistemic power and privilege. Amplifying the testimonies of marginalized speakers is not the same thing as marginalized speakers having credibility in our own right and on our own terms. Evolving epistemic frameworks are determined by the boundaries and limitations that exist for marginalized knowers *within* the confines of dominant knowing. They are also predicated on how sympathetic dominant knowers choose to engage with marginalized knowers on projects of mutual concern. Evolving frameworks may help challenge the hegemony of dominant knowing by elevating and/or amplifying marginalized epistemic resources—in this sense, they are decent but not perfect candidates for addressing willful ignorance— but they rarely impact longstanding relations of social and epistemic power. As I will argue in chapter 5, evolving frameworks are primarily forms of *epistemic charity*. Epistemic charity does not demand that those with social power and identity power renounce that power. Instead it relies on minimal social or epistemic sacrifice on the part of sympathetic dominant knowers. For this reason, evolving frameworks almost always dissolve in the face of pressure from the wider epistemic landscape.

Another issue that arises with evolving epistemic frameworks is that marginalized knowers are often used as passive experts or *situational* epistemic experts. I use the term "passive expert" to describe situations where marginalized knowers are considered to have a kind of epistemic authority over a localized set of social experiences but that authority pertains almost exclusively to issues of marginalization. (There are strong echoes of this view within standpoint theory as well.) Passive expertise is also passive in terms of social power as the conferral of expertise, and by extension credibility, can be revoked by those with greater social power. Active expertise *also* arises from epistemic authority over a localized set of experiences but that that expertise is bolstered, as opposed to hindered, by the possession of social power. Active experts do not have to worry about having their expertise challenged within evolving frameworks because social power still dictates credibility, credibility that can, in turn, circumscribe marginalized knowing within an evolving framework. For example, in the case of the Never Again movement, trans women of color pointed out that the Never Again manifesto, written to inspire new gun reform legislation, encouraged the disclosure of mental health information to law enforcement despite the dangers that it presented to the trans community. Although there were marginalized knowers who could have better informed the manifesto, their concepts and epistemic resources were not included. As Lourdes Hunter, director of the Trans Women of Color

Collective noted, "not that I expected it to be, but [the] manifesto just wasn't informed or aligned with people who are most disproportionately impacted by gun violence and state-sanctioned violence. Period" (Alexander 2018).

The role of social power in creating and maintaining evolving epistemic frameworks is one of the primary reasons why the frameworks are so unstable. Asymmetrical power relations and a reliance on passive expertise undermines the larger goal of amplifying marginalized knowing. Consider a common refrain in social justice movements that more dominantly situated knowers ought not "speak for" marginalized knowers. The argument is that the power asymmetry between dominant knowers and marginalized knowers makes it problematic for dominant knowers to speak to and about marginalized social experiences. One goal of amplification is to cede dominant public space in order to allow marginalized testimonies and resources to come forward, not to utilize that space as a dominant participant representing marginalized perspectives. That said, there is a difference between not speaking for others and relying on marginalized knowers to decode social experiences of violence and oppression for dominant knowers. The former may find reasonable justification but that latter almost assuredly will not. This is because relying on marginalized knowers to be passive experts of what are essentially *shared* social experiences reinforces the dominant view of marginalized social experiences and epistemic resources as somehow *unknowable*. As I suggested in the last chapter, this type of willful ignorance is very hard to maintain as our social experiences and social lives are shared and deeply intertwined. Willful ignorance simply becomes another way of confirming a lack of interest in one's own life and the experiences that give it shape, a distressing hallmark of social and epistemic privilege

The New Yorker writer, Emily Witt, notes how the Never Again organizers relied on marginalized groups like Chicago's Peace Warriors to speak to and for gun violence in Black communities but consistently refused to engage with the social experiences of Black victims of gun violence in the mainstream media. Instead they collectively shrugged their shoulders, invoking the argument that "they didn't know" about such experiences and thus should not be the ones to talk about them. Pointing, instead, to the Peace Warriors as passive experts. Never Again activist, David Hogg, argued that the reason that they did not speak for, or on behalf of marginalized victims of gun violence, particularly Black victims of gun violence and Native American victims of gun violence, was because the organizers' experiences of suburban gun violence was not like the violence that occurred in other communities (Witt 2018). He invoked the dissimilarity of experience as grounds for remaining silent despite the fact that the necessary epistemic resources were readily available in the form of marginalized testimonies. Hogg's claim reinforces the idea that the social experiences of marginalized knowers are critically unrelated to the social experiences of dominant knowers thus justifying their willful refusal to know.

But, as Witt asks, "What example did it set if the Parkland students, with all of their radical empathy, treated [marginalized social experiences of] violence as unknowable?" (2018). What epistemic opportunities are lost when public space is ceded to marginalized knowers but the chance to learn and employ marginalized epistemic resources is still willfully avoided? This is not an issue of *unknowability* but an issue of failed epistemic responsibility. Hogg does not claim that being in a dominant social location makes it epistemically *irresponsible* for him to speak on behalf of marginalized knowers but that he cannot speak because he "doesn't know" about marginalized social experiences. He fails to see that the social experiences that he subdivides by demographics, locations, and ethnicities are, in fact, shared experiences of violence in the United States. Thus he fails to know critical features of his own social experiences. It may be the case that speaking for marginalized knowers is still problematic even when dominant knowers *do* engage with marginalized epistemic resources. This argument, as characterized by Alcoff, goes roughly like this: speaking for others is *always* wrong because social location impacts the meaning and truth of our assertions such that privileged social locations can be "discursively dangerous" in cases where more privileged knowers speak for less privileged knowers (1991, 7). If it is true that social location can make it "discursively dangerous" to speak, then, of course it is wrong to criticize dominant knowers for failing to do so.

However, Alcoff argues, the problem of speaking for others cannot be resolved by requiring that knowers speak only from and *for* the groups in which they belong. Such strategies merely raise and different set of troubling questions. "For example, we might ask, if I don't speak for those less privileged than myself, am I abandoning my political responsibility to speak out against oppression, a responsibility incurred by the very fact of my privilege?," Alcoff asks, "If I should not speak for others, should I restrict myself to following their lead uncritically? Is my greatest contribution to *move over and get out of the way*? And if so, what is the best way to do this–to keep silent or to deconstruct my discourse?" (1991, 8). Alcoff argues that the claim that knowers ought to speak only for themselves and not for others runs contrary to the idea that we all create "public, discursive" selves *for ourselves* and public, discursive selves for *others as well* (1991, 10). Pretending that wholly autonomous selves exist allows dominant knowers to distance themselves from their role in upholding dominant discourses. It also allows dominant knowers to retreat into their own worldviews for self-interested reasons or to avoid "discursive imperialism" (Alcoff 1991, 17). The idea that we only "speak for ourselves" can be problematically self-serving and materially dangerous for vulnerable and marginalized others. "There is no neutral place to stand free and clear in which one's words do not prescriptively affect or mediate the experience of others," Alcoff argues, "nor is there a way to decisively demarcate a boundary between one's location and all others. Even a complete retreat from speech is of course not neutral since it allows the continued dominance of current discourses and acts by omission to reinforce their dominance" (1991, 20). Citing Gayatri Spivak's "Can the Subaltern Speak?," she suggests that instead of *speaking for* marginalized knowers, socially dominant knowers should aim to *speak to* and *speak with* socially marginalized knowers (Alcoff 1991, 23). This does not mean that there is no political role for *speaking for* marginalized knowers, if performed with care, but that speaking for marginalized knowers should first begin with due caution ("The impetus to speak must be carefully analyzed and, in many cases (certainly for academics!), fought against) (Alcoff 1991, 24).

Sympathetic dominant knowers and dominant allies should explicitly investigate how social context and social location impact what they want to say. They should also keep in mind that they are both accountable to and responsible for what is said. They should look to what their speech *does* in the world, what it performs ("where the speech goes and what it does there"), and know that speech itself is not neutral with regard to its operations (Alcoff 1991, 27). It is true that *speaking for* is socially and epistemically fraught and may serve only to reinforce problematic social hierarchies, but, as Alcoff concludes, citing Loyce Stewart, sometimes the testimonies of marginalized knowers need a messenger (1991, 29). In evolving epistemic frameworks, there is an important secondary role for speaking for marginalized knowers, particularly in terms of how dominant knowers speak to *other* dominant knowers outside of the evolving framework. This role, I will argue in chapter 5, is critical in terms of structural efforts to dismantle the hegemony of dominant knowing as it will require dominant knowers to come to know themselves better such that they can *know better.* At the conclusion of Witt's article, she asks if dominant knowers could ever be trusted to listen to the social experiences of marginalized knowers and to see those experiences as part of *shared* social problems (2018). She essentially asks if dominant knowers will ever challenge their own willful ignorance in order to work in conjunction with marginalized for better, more inclusive futures—futures uncoupled from the injustice and oppression of dominant knowing.

I am tempted to respond that our collective problems of injustice, both epistemic and social, are more nuanced than we think and more repairable than we think. At the level of individuals, I think we ought to let go of remedies that rely on interrupting bias and prejudice; however, at the level of collectives, I think we ought to push further for interruptions and investigations into willful ignorance. The remaining problem, as I see it, is that interrupting willful ignorance cannot be based on extensions of epistemic good will or charity. That is what happens in the case of evolving epistemic frameworks and, as we can see, it is not always successful. If resolving willful ignorance will help remove the burden of testimonial injustice and epistemic labor for marginalized knowers, then we need to find a way to do so in ways that move beyond temporary frameworks for collective meaning-making. Remediation measures need to be built into social structures and systems such that we are redistributing social and epistemic power between dominant knowers and marginalized knowers. In chapter 5, I consider what is perhaps the most difficult part of this project, theorizing the shift from individual, agent-based interventions into epistemic injustice to large-scale social interventions in ways that promote large-scale epistemic redress while avoiding dominant reactionary pushback.

NOTES

1. See also Devine and Monteith (1993). "The Role of Discrepancy-Associated Affect in Prejudice Reduction," in *Affect, Cognition and Stereotyping: Interactive Processes in Group Perception*, eds., D. M. Mackie & D. L. Hamilton. San Diego: Academic Press, pp. 317–344.

2. See also Kawakami, Dovidio, Moll, Hermsen, and Russin (2000).

3. The Shooter Task refers to a computer simulation experiment where images of black and white males appear on a screen holding a gun or a non-gun object. Study participants are given a short response time and tasked with pressing a button, or "shooting" armed images versus unarmed images. Psychological studies have revealed a "shooter bias" in the tendency to shoot black, unarmed males more often than unarmed white males. See Correll, Park, Wittenbrink, and Judd (2002).

4. A "messy environment" presents additional challenges to studies like the one discussed here. As Kees Keizer, Siegwart Lindenberg, and Linda Steg (2008) claim in "The Spreading of Disorder," people are more likely to violate social rules when they see that others are violating the rules as well. I can only imagine that this is applicable to *epistemic rules* as well. I mention this here to suggest that the "cleanliness" of the social environment of social psychological studies such as the one by Mendoza, Saaid, Gollwitzer, Peter, and Amodio, David (2010) presents an additional obstacle in extrapolating the resulting behaviors of research participants to the public-at-large. Short of mass hypnosis, how could the strategies used in these experiments, strategies that are predicated on the noninterference of other destabilizing factors, be meaningfully applied to everyday life? There is a tendency in the philosophical literature on implicit bias and stereotype threat to outright ignore the limited applicability of much of this research in order to make critical claims about interventions into racist, sexist, homophobic, and transphobic behaviors. Philosophers would do well to recognize the complexity of these issues and to be more cautious about the enthusiastic endorsement of experimental results.

5. See Webb, Sheeran, and Pepper (2012).

6. Of this "rogue" group, Glaser and Knowles note: "This group had, on average, a negative RWS (i.e., rather than just a low bias toward Blacks, they tended to associate Whites more than Blacks with weapons; see footnote 4). If these reversed stereotypes are also uninhibited, they should yield reversed Shooter Bias, as observed here" (2007, 169).

7. See Fielder, Messner, and Bluemke (2006) ; Brendl, Markman, and Messner (2001) ; Fazio and Olson (2003).

8. There is significant debate over the issue of whether the implicit bias that IAT tests claim to measure actually translate into real-world discriminatory behavior. This is a complex and compelling issue that could potentially render moot most discussion of IAT tests. As Anthony G. Greenwald, Mahzarin R. Banaji, and Brian A. Nosek write: "Implicit Association Test (IAT) measures have two properties that render them problematic to use to classify persons as likely to engage in discrimination. Those two properties are modest test–retest reliability (for the Implicit Association Test (IAT), typically between r = .5 and r = .6; cf., Nosek et al., 2007) and small to moderate predictive validity effect sizes. Therefore, attempts to diagnostically use such measures for individuals risk undesirably high rates of erroneous classifications. These problems of limited test-retest reliability and small effect sizes are maximal when the sample consists of a single person (i.e., for individual diagnostic use), but they diminish substantially as sample size increases. Therefore, limited reliability and small to moderate effect sizes are not problematic in diagnosing system-level discrimination, for which analyses often involve large samples" (2015, 557). Additionally, Oswald et al. argue that "Implicit Association Test (IAT) scores correlated strongly with measures of brain activity but relatively weakly with all other criterion measures in the race domain and weakly with all criterion measures in the ethnicity domain. IATs, whether they were designed to tap into implicit prejudice or implicit stereotypes, were typically poor predictors of the types of behavior, judgments, or decisions that have been studied as instances of discrimination, regardless of how subtle, spontaneous, controlled, or deliberate they were. Explicit measures of bias were also, on average, weak predictors of criteria in the studies covered by this meta-analysis, but explicit measures performed no worse than, and sometimes better than, the IATs for predictions of policy preferences, interpersonal behavior, person perceptions, reaction times, and microbehavior. Only for brain activity were correlations higher for IATs than for explicit measures . . . but few studies examined prediction of brain activity using explicit measures. Any distinction between the IATs and explicit measures is a distinction that makes little difference, because both of these means of measuring attitudes resulted in poor prediction of racial and ethnic discrimination" (2013, 182–183). For further details about this debate, see Oswald, Mitchell, Blanton, Jaccard, and Tetlock (2013) and Greenwald, Banaji, and Nosek (2015).

9. See Oswald, Mitchell, Blanton, Jaccard, and Tetlock (2015).

10. In Green's article, Marjory Stoneman Douglas High School junior, Tyah-Amoy Roberts, noted that The Black Lives Matter movement has been invested in issues of gun violence since the 2012 murder of Trayvon Martin but the mainstream media was unwilling to consider it an important social issue until it was addressed by the mostly white Parkland students (2018). See also Kelkar (2018).

Chapter 5

Epistemic Charity, Epistemic Standpoints, and Structural Epistemic Justice

In the last chapter, I explored ways of interrupting willful ignorance. I appealed to the epistemology of disagreement as a mechanism of interruption because disagreement should, at least initially, make dominant knowers less confident in the status of their own beliefs. However, addressing willful ignorance in this way requires that dominant knowers be able to engage in disagreement in non-identity prejudicial ways. Disagreement tends to fail as a mechanism of interruption because it requires subjective assessments of epistemic peerhood and/or subjective assessments of epistemic superiority or inferiority while having no bird's-eye-view from which to make such assessments. It allows for unjust credibility deflations and unjust assignments of epistemic inferiority to negatively impact the process. This makes sense, of course, considering that disagreement falls within the category of testimony and is also subject to forms of testimonial injustice. The hope with disagreement, though—as opposed to general incidents of testimony—is that disagreement itself will heighten dominant knowers' sensitivity to the accuracy/inaccuracy of their beliefs. That said, and as I noted regarding testimonial virtue in Chapter 1, this may not be the case in practice. In fact, we have no reason to think that *epistemic* concerns, say, about evidence or the accuracy of our beliefs, can override cognitive dispositions toward bias and prejudice. Disagreement may give dominant knowers cause to dive a bit deeper into the reasons it goes wrong, but this far from guaranteed.

That aside, following a call by Miranda Fricker and Jennifer Saul, I still considered some recent work in social psychology on methods and strategies for mitigating implicit bias and prejudice. I offered a brief overview of some common models for mitigating implicit bias, finding, in most cases, that the models lacked good evidence for real-world applicability. Furthermore, it remains very unclear how data-driven mitigation strategies can aid in resolving the kinds of persistent racial and gender biases that pervade the everyday experiences of marginalized knowers. Instead, I suggested that it may be more useful to think about addressing willful ignorance by way of collective epistemic spaces—evolving epistemic frameworks—where dominant knowers and marginalized knowers pursue projects of mutual concern. Evolving frameworks offer spaces for dominant knowers to engage with marginalized epistemic resources and to potentially learn to hear and know across hermeneutical divides. The upshot of these frameworks is that sympathetic dominant knowers take an *active interest* in marginalized epistemic resources, that is, they *want to engage* and to do so in thoughtful ways. The problem is that the frameworks do not require actual social-structural change and are thus often plagued by issues of willful ignorance and related problems of social power. These are the very problems the frameworks hoped to solve. Evolving frameworks also tend to revert back to the dominant status quo along with any extensions of credibility and/or amplifications that they conferred to marginalized knowers.

In this chapter, I suggest that marginalized knowers cannot rely on extensions of good will or charity by sympathetic dominant knowers in order to realize epistemic justice. This is because epistemic charity does not require that dominant knowers sacrifice any of the social power and identity power that keeps dominant knowing in place. The willingness of sympathetic dominant knowers and dominant allies to engage in social and epistemic justice-oriented policies and projects is offered as a type of non-binding contract. Dominant knowers may extricate themselves from the contract, change the terms, or dissolve the contract altogether at their convenience. We may be able to avoid epistemic charity by focusing instead on marginalized social locations and the privileging of marginalized standpoints. This is methodologically related to the use of evolving epistemic frameworks but invokes two controversial theses that may make a stronger case for the interruption of willful ignorance: 1) the thesis of essentialism and 2) the thesis of automatic epistemic privilege. I try to unpack whether a reimagining of these two theses could provide a better, and less corruptible, mechanism to address willful ignorance and, ultimately, testimonial injustice and epistemic labor.

In the second part of this chapter, I argue that, unfortunately, standpoints often prove as temporary and fragile as evolving epistemic framework. This is because the adoption of a standpoint as social and epistemic practice is also ultimately dictated by the dominant knowers' desire to engage accordingly with marginalized knowers, or rather, it is merely another form of epistemic charity. The epistemic advantages accrued to standpoints can be rejected or revoked at the dominant knowers' discretion. So, in the third part of this chapter, I consider a final strategy, one that aims to relocate assessments of credibility away from individual dominant knowers and into social structures and social institutions. The hope is that the structural pursuit of epistemic justice will better address that pervasive harms of persistent testimonial injustice and epistemic labor and will circumvent, in critical ways, the difficulties of battling entrenched willful ignorance. Here I look to Elizabeth Anderson's work on epistemic justice as a virtue of institutions, Nancy Arden McHugh's work on communities of epistemic resistance, and Michael Doan's work on resisting structural epistemic injustice.

The benefit of thinking institutionally is, I claim, threefold: (1) epistemic justice can be reframed as a wider sociopolitical issue beyond individual epistemic practices and matters of individual virtue, sympathy, or charity, (2) marginalized knowers will have a wider range of institutional policies, practices, and values to appeal to in order to remediate individual issues of testimonial injustice and epistemic labor, and (3) marginalized knowers will be able to root claims of willful ignorance or "non-knowing" on the part of dominant knowers in failures of institutions to incorporate marginalized epistemic resources into their creation, maintenance, and daily operation, effectively externalizing claims of willful ignorance. Although these measures will not absolve individual dominant knowers from charges of epistemic injustice and willful ignorance, it will ground the necessary epistemic resources into more facets of our daily lives. It will also help us move away from accounts of epistemic injustice that rely on the motivation of dominant knowers to "do the right thing" and to focus our attention on building and maintaining the social structures that allow the "right thing" to be a matter of course and not a matter of individual choice. The benefit of theorizing institutional or structural epistemic justice is to further reorient discussions away from the practices of individual dominant knowers and to center the theories and practices that marginalized communities use to actualize our own epistemic agency and advocate for our own sociopolitical agendas *on our own terms*.

I focus first on the concept of epistemic charity as a way of broadly discussing epistemic remediation measures for epistemic injustice that rely on individual good will, sympathy, virtue or right motivation, to resolve problems of persistent epistemic injustice and epistemic labor. Charity is a commendable practice but a poor method of remediation because it does not necessitate that the charitable party meaningfully engage in correcting the background injustices that lead to the call for charity in the first place. We can think of epistemic charity as broadly stemming from a Western concept of religious charity and the Christian New Testament call to "love thy neighbor as thyself." This religious precept is often interpreted as either a religious virtue in the vein of Saint Thomas Aquinas's theological virtues, virtues that we come to know by divine revelation, or as extensions of religious dogma, as rules or codes of behavior ordained by a Christian God. In both cases, the practice of charity arises from something like the "Golden Rule" or the idea that one ought to treat others as they themselves would like to be treated. Over time the practice of charity has been importantly disconnected—although not entirely disconnected—from its religious origins and has taken on the characteristics of a performative social good like performing one's civic duties or engaging in public service, e.g., voting, volunteering, etc.

However, unlike other performative social goods, the aim of charity is not to change background social conditions or to remedy social injustice. Instead, charity is based on attending to the needs of others *because of* background social conditions. Charity exists because our social and political structures fail to attend adequately to the needs of others. Charity typically attends to the lack of material goods or the ability to obtain or manage material goods. It does not consider a just redistribution of goods to be its primary object of concern (thus making charity itself unnecessary) but the distribution of additional goods within an unjust system. For example, one might donate to individuals after the wreckage of a natural disaster, or to families suffering famine after a war, but this does little to affect the background reasons of why the wreckage was particularly acute or why the violent conflicts began in the first place. One particularly pointed example is found in the rise of crowdfunding websites like GoFundMe or JustGiving, websites that facilitate online charitable donations to those who have suffered from a range of misfortunes like police violence, sudden job loss, or devastating hospital bills after a health crisis. In these cases, we can see clearly how charity exists directly alongside the social and political systems that originate these misfortunes and then subsequently fail to take care of people in the aftermath.

Epistemic charity works in a similar fashion. Epistemic injustice assumes that there is an unjust distribution of epistemic credibility or unjust access to epistemic goods and resources that can be ameliorated on an individual basis with extensions of credibility and/or improved access to epistemic goods and resources (and the creation of said resources). Epistemic injustice does not assume that unjust distributions of epistemic goods and resources requires demands a fair or just redistribution of those goods and resources such that epistemic injustice fails to obtain in the first place. That is why it is easier to conceptualize epistemic justice as dependent on something like epistemic virtue instead. Any fair and just redistribution of epistemic goods and resources would involve the restructuring of the social and political systems that underwrite the distribution of those goods. We would have to restructure the systems of social power and identity power that give rise to epistemic injustice. Epistemic charity, on the other hand, only requires that dominant knowers extend themselves as much as they can in cases where they consciously recognize negative identity prejudice affecting their credibility assessments of others. For example, dominant knowers might try to mitigate testimonial injustice by employing testimonial virtue and inflating the credibility of marginalized speakers but they are *not* asked to address the corrupt origins of social power that created the situation in which they find themselves. This is because at no point are the background social conditions of epistemic injustice, i.e., the social power to confer credibility, addressed by the remediation measures that most views epistemic justice endorse. Dominant knowers are not asked to sacrifice the social power or identity power that they have unjustly acquired or *even asked to question* the power that they have to deflate the credibility of marginalized knowers. Instead, testimonial virtue, like epistemic charity, merely asks dominant knowers to offer something that they have in more than sufficient supply, the ability to extend or withdraw credibility at their discretion.

Dominant knowing and dominant resources are unjust because they are dependent on dominant social structures that are themselves unjust. It may be the case that we can pull apart epistemic injustice originating from unjust social power from the unjust social structures that *confer* that social power but it is not clear to me that this is at all possible. The social power that underwrites epistemic power is based upon long histories of social and economic violence and oppression against marginalized others. The severity of historical oppression and marginalization is different for different social groups and exists along a gradient. There is no linear pathway by which we can consider histories of social oppression and corresponding epistemic oppression that will not demand looking closely at specific communities and social histories, patterns of migration (forced and unforced), social assimilation, and economic and political inclusion and exclusion. How social power gives rise to epistemic power, how these systems rely on each other, and the extent to which they rely on each other is an open question. But the fact that social power *does* bestow epistemic power, and specifically the power to extend and withdraw credibility, does not seem up for debate. It is tempting to suggest that we should not, or cannot, implicate dominant knowers in unjust knowing across all knowledge claims but that is only an attempt to carve out the epistemic landscape without considering how that landscape was formed. If knowledge claims hinge to social power in the way that I am suggesting, then this implicates *all* knowledge claims across the entirety of our social experiences, even the seemingly benign ones, e.g., "It is raining in Boston today." There are cases that will be more benign than others and there are cases that will be more severe than others but that does not mean that there are cases that fail to be infected by social power. Consider that *whom* we believe upon hearing, "It is raining in Boston today," and *why* we believe them are directly influenced by socialized perceptions of credibility. Extensions of epistemic credibility move through the same conduits as social power and so any remediation of unjust extensions of credibility must do the same. That is why epistemic charity constitutes such a fundamentally flawed endeavor; it fails to attend to the redistribution of epistemic power and thus fails to intervene in epistemic injustice in a consistent and lasting manner.

We might try replacing the concept of epistemic charity with a concept of *epistemic priority* or *epistemic privilege* for marginalized knowers. Epistemic priority and epistemic privilege invoke the standpoint thesis that the situatedness or social location of marginalized knowers is an epistemically advantaged position. This is because standpoint theorists argue that what we can know is determined by our social location; our location sets the boundaries of our perspective. Standpoint theorists recognize that how society is arranged, and the degree of social inequality that it permits, shapes how we come to see and understand the world. As Lorraine Code notes in rejecting positive-empiricist epistemologies, and as I have echoed here, there is no "view from nowhere," or no wholly objective position from which we can begin and end inquiry (1993, 16). In socially stratified societies, those with the social position to shape inquiry and methods of inquiry are often unaware of how their social power naturalizes and universalizes those inquiries and methods. Marginalized knowers are in a better position to understand the influence of social power and identity power on both perceptions of credibility, and the non-epistemic interests that shape the wider epistemic landscape, because social oppression demands knowing one's oppressor. As I argued in the context of epistemic labor, there are consequences of "knowing wrong" for marginalized knowers. The development of double-consciousness, or double-knowing, is a necessary survival strategy for this reason. Standpoint theorists like Sandra Harding argue that knowledge produced from the marginalized perspective can lead to *greater* objectivity because, unlike dominant knowing, it is not unduly influenced by the idea that its partial perspective is the universal perspective. Harding calls this view, *strong objectivity*. In one of her most well-known pieces on standpoint epistemology, she writes:

> The starting point of standpoint theory—and its claim that is most often misread—is that in societies stratified by race, ethnicity, class, gender, sexuality, or some other such politics shaping the very structure of a society, the *activities* of those at the top both organize and set limits on what persons who perform such activities can understand about themselves and the world around them. "There are some perspectives on society from which, however well-intentioned one may be, the real relations of humans with each other and with the natural world are not visible." In contrast, the activities of those at the bottom of such social hierarchies can provide starting points for thought—for *everyone's* research and scholarship—from which humans' relations with each other and the natural world can become visible. This is because the experience and lives of marginalized peoples, as they understand them, provide particularly significant *problems to be explained* or research agendas. (Harding 1993, 54)

Critics of standpoint theory argue that it confers epistemic priority or epistemic privilege on to marginalized knowers in ways that lead to greater plurality of perspectives but not necessarily to greater objectivity. As Helen Longino argues, it is entirely possible that a multiplicity of perspectives never converges to give us a more complex, truth-oriented perspective. "However much I and they inform ourselves about one another's life situations we can neither share nor escape our social locations unless we materially dismantle them," she argues, "and even then we cannot escape our histories. There is, therefore, no guarantee of a convergence of theory, even when it meets Harding's criterion for maximal objectivity" (Longino 1993a, 211–212). The worry is that focusing on marginalized perspectives will not necessarily bring us closer to the truth but will instead reify essentialist models of social groups and unquestioned attributions of epistemic authority. Alison Wylie identifies the following as untenable theses of standpoint theory: (1) *essentialism,* or the claim that there are no essential attributes that all members of a social group share thus no clear social kinds in which to ground "standpoints," and (2) the *inversion thesis*, or the claim that epistemic priority or privilege constitutes a kind of "automatic epistemic privilege" by virtue of social location irrespective of "knowing how things really are" (2012, 59). To make the concept of epistemic privilege work, we need to either justify essentialism and the inversion thesis as necessary to a working standpoint epistemology or to reject both theses as outdated interpretations.

Essentialism insists that if there are no attributes or properties that all members of a group share, or no generalizable categories of experience that apply to all members alike, then we cannot adequately mark the boundaries of a social group. For instance, in theorizing the concept of *woman,* we may create categories of experience that map on to some women's lives while omitting the experiences of other women and, as a result, radically underdetermining appeals to women's standpoints:

> In making the case that "one is not born, but rather becomes a woman," as Beauvoir famously put it (1952, 249), feminists themselves had effectively demonstrated the contingency and diversity of women's roles and identities; if the category "woman" has no anchor in essential attributes shared by all of its members, what basis could there be for appeals to a woman's or feminist "standpoint," or for that matter, any social identity-defined standpoint? (Wylie 2012, 59)

Essentialism demands that there be deep enough commonalities in within-group experiences as to group people into social kinds. However, the wide variety of within-group experiences makes that demand implausible in practice. But clearly there are meaningful ways to talk about social identities and social groups that do not require an essentialist commitment of this stripe. Members of social groups may also have shared histories and *other* common-alities that mark membership in the group. For example, shared histories of social oppression and social injustice mark members of marginalized social groups as either epistemically advantaged or epistemically disadvantaged, and it is by way of these histories that we can call individual knowers epis-temically advantaged or disadvantaged. A revised notion of essentialism can ground standpoints and preserve the notion of social identities and social groups without being wedded to claims of necessarily shared attributes. A revised notion of essentialism may also allow knowers to belong to many different social groups, with intersecting, hybrid social identities, in relations that are political, historical, and fluid.

Alison Wylie and Sergio Sismondo claim, citing the work Alcoff (2006) and Paula Moya and Michael Hames-García (2000), that essentialist claims of social identity need not make metaphysical claims about identity in order to generate legitimate epistemic standpoints: "collective identities do not have to be 'quasi-universal' to give rise to distinctive bodies of experience and perspective that can mobilize a critical standpoint on oppressive structures" (2015). There are other social, historical, and positional factors that lead to the construction of social identities and other systemic inequalities and injus-tices that create social groups from intersecting histories of social-historical violence and oppression. "The conventional terms of the debate over essen-tialism are thought by many to have been mistaken in their ahistorical, falsely homogenized account of what essentialism as a concept or a doctrine entails," Alcoff argues, "If the essentialists were guilty of overly homogenizing the category of women, the anti-essentialists were guilty of overly homogeniz-ing the category or idea of essentialism" (2006, 152). Essentialism can be a more flexible philosophical thesis than its quick dismissal often suggests. As Alcoff writes, "essentialism can coexist with nominalism and even histori-cism, since it is a doctrine about essences but not a doctrine about the meta-physical grounds or stability of those essences" (2006, 152). The appeal of essentialism divorced from metaphysical presumptions is that it can coalesce shared social experiences which can, in turn, be used as a locus for social and political engagement with other social groups. The drawback, however, lies in our tendency to overdetermine and over-ascribe attributes to members of a social group such that we solidify and concretize those attributes, flattening and masking intragroup differences, failing to capture how social identities and social groups change over time.

A revised notion of essentialism that focuses on shared histories and social experiences may alleviate some of the critical concerns with standpoint meth-ods but may also miss elements of social identity that *are* tied to other socio-cultural preoccupations with the shared biological properties of particular groups. Although biological properties do not make a group what it is—as our social concepts too often incorrectly and unjustly hinge to biological properties—the possession of certain biological properties can be correlated with distinct social and historical experiences like race-based and gender-based violence and oppression. While we cannot ignore histories of abuses against marginalized and oppressed people *because* of the possession of specific biological properties, e.g., melanocytes, chromosomes, this does not mean that the possession of such properties uniquely determines social identity or makes an individual what they are in an ontological sense. Biological properties cannot fix a knower in the social world. Rather, we can identify certain biological properties as related to social identities, or social groups, where the possession (or lack of possession) of those properties is characteristic of, but not synonymous with, patterned social histories. Biological properties are part of a complex matrix of other social properties that contribute to the "what it's like" to occupy certain social identities or social groups. There is something that *it is like* to live in a dark-skinned body, or a cisgender body, or a transgender body that maps onto a whole host of shared social experiences and social histories. These can contribute to one's own sense of belonging to a certain social identity or social group as well. We can see this in the first few lines of Shirley J. Scott's 1963 article, "The Negro Walks on Eggshells," as she attempts to describe the "what it's like" to be Black in America:

> Imagine, if you can, your skin not white but black. Imagine your present job, education and income the same, but your family shades of brown . . .
>
> You worry over the possibility of war, you complain about taxes, you pay the rent and grocery bill . . .
>
> Then how different are you from other men? Are you different? . . .
>
> You don't feel different, yet you are treated differently. You can't justify the treatment accorded you, but you must live and cope with white justification. (1963)

As Scott describes, the possession of dark or brown skin correlates with both social identity and with particular patterns of social treatment by other dominant social groups. To be clear, I am not claiming that the possession of brown skin as a biological property is *all there is* to the social concept of race or race-based treatment. Race is a much more fluid and flexible concept. It works in ways that can, and certainly does, track different properties at different times and to different degrees. Consider, for example, the historical relationship between the degree of African ancestry and its relationship to whiteness in the United States, e.g., the historical transition from the "one-drop rule" to mixed-race, or multiracial, identities. The point is that there *are* biological properties that track, albeit not neatly, racial and gender identities in ways that construct our social identities and social group membership. As Alcoff writes:

> One's racial and gender identity is fundamental to one's social and familial interactions. It contributes to one's perspective on events—to one's interpretation of conversations, media reports, and social theories—and it determines in large part one's status within the community and the way in which a great deal of what one says and does is interpreted by others. Thus, our "visible" and acknowledged identity affects our relations in the world, which in turn affects our interior life, that is, our lived experiences or subjectivity. If social identities such as race and gender are fundamental in this way to one's experiences, then it only makes sense to say that they are fundamental to the self. (2006, 92)

If we take essentialism to capture a more flexible and dynamic set of properties and attributes, and deny the stronger metaphysical view of essentialism, then perhaps we can ground standpoints, or epistemic privilege, in social identity or social groups without issue. We can reorient inquiry and methods of inquiry from the perspective of marginalized social groups while still committing to the notion that social identity and social group membership are internally diverse and can shift and change over time. The question then becomes should marginalized perspectives, or marginalized standpoints, be granted something like unreflective or automatic epistemic privilege? This is the second untenable thesis of standpoint theory. As Kristina Rolin argues, the inversion thesis, or the thesis of epistemic privilege, is criticized because it "does not provide any standards of epistemic justification that enable one to judge some socially grounded perspectives as better than others," and that "it is not clear either *what kind of evidence* we should expect in support of the thesis of epistemic privilege" (2006, 125–126, my italics). For example, it seems difficult to justify how an uneducated or undereducated subsistence farmer in the Global South is in a better position to know about the economic dangers of agribusiness in the Americas *because* of their position on the margins. There is "no guarantee that the experience of oppression or marginality will, in itself, generate critical and constructive insights of these kinds," Wylie and Sismondo argue, as "systems of oppression impose significant epistemic deficits on those they disadvantage" (2015). These deficits include lack of literacy, education, and a wider understanding of the systems of oppression that underwrite one's own experiences: "Strong readings of the 'inversion' thesis are, then, clearly untenable: comprehensive epistemic 'privilege' cannot be attributed automatically to those who are oppressed just because they are oppressed" (Wylie and Sismondo 2015).

Furthermore, echoing Rolin's concern, Wylie and Sismondo argue that standpoint theory cannot justify privileging some standpoints over others or taking some standpoints as more objective than others. There is also the concern that the situated knowledge thesis and the thesis of epistemic privilege are contradictory bedfellows. If all knowledge is partial, then how can we justify privileging *some* partial knowledge as more objective than others? This is *the bias paradox*: "As Helen Longino explains, in order to argue that some socially grounded perspectives are better than others, a standpoint epistemologist would have to be able to identify privileged perspectives from a non-interested position, but according to standpoint epistemology, there is no such position" (Rolin 2006, 126). Rolin attempts to satisfy the bias paradox by way of a contextualist approach to epistemic justification. Following Michael Williams, Rolin's argues that if we take marginalized standpoints as default entitlements, or beliefs that we hold until asked to defend them with evidence, the bias paradox will not arise. This is because the bias paradox relies on the foundationalist claim that there *is* a "view from nowhere" imagined as a set of basic beliefs that have the same epistemic status in every context (Rolin 2006, 129). Instead, she argues, default entitlements are situated knowledge claims, although they may appear in multiple contexts, they are not the same in every context, "therefore, if we adopt contextualism, there is no contradiction between the thesis of epistemic privilege and the situated knowledge thesis" (Rolin 2006, 129).

Still, the contextualist position appears only to kick the can down the road. It assumes that when a knower's beliefs are challenged in a particular context that we will have some independent or objective means of adjudicating that challenge, but if our knowledge claims are partial and situated, then how could that be the case? In the context discussed here, if the evidence justifying a marginalized knowledge claim is challenged, then on what grounds are we arriving at an objective conclusion about the status of that evidence, particularly as there is no objective vantage point from which we can proceed? What happens when we disagree about what constitutes evidence or how that evidence should be interpreted? Williams's notes, much like Lorraine Code, that there are normative demands on knowledge such that we ought to be epistemically responsible in attuning to evidence and calls to revise upon new evidence (2001, 13–14). However, the fact that evidential demands can shift and change between contexts—or that we could fail to agree about evidence—makes calls for epistemic responsibility too hollow. This issue becomes particularly acute when considering that our assessment of evidence may also fail to be neutral due to identity prejudice or willful ignorance (see chapter 3). The main problem with invoking Williams's contextualism as a defense against the bias paradox is that contextualism is itself a situated knowledge thesis thus it is not clear how Rolin's argument can avoid begging the question. Epistemic privilege as a means to more objective epistemic ends seems implausible, but, as some standpoint theorists claim, this does not mean that marginalized perspectives fail to be epistemically useful:

> Not surprisingly, then, standpoint theorists typically construe the metaphor of privilege in terms of possibilities for understanding. As reformulated in response to critiques of essentialism and relativism, standpoint theory is best understood as a conceptual framework, an open-ended set of analytic resources, for addressing jointly descriptive and normative questions about the epistemic effects of oppression (Wylie 2012). Its point of departure is a situated knowledge thesis: one that presumes the epistemic relevance of systemic conditions of inequality without specifying in advance what their relevance will be in a given context. It directs attention to asymmetries in epistemic circumstance which suggest that important epistemic advantages (not privilege) may contingently accrue to those who are oppressed (Wylie and Sismondo 2015).

Wylie claims that standpoints are best understood as an epistemic position knowers adopt in contexts where epistemic inequality generated by social oppression biases research questions and/or research agendas. In these contexts, marginalized perspectives, or standpoints, may prove to be epistemically advantageous but not *automatically* so. Notice that the recognition and adoption of a standpoint, or marginalized perspective, involves at least one layer of assessment or judgment about which groups qualify as having a legitimate standpoint in the first place. Standpoint theory thus seems to permit another internal hierarchy to emerge. We can recognize that standpoints are socially fluid and internally diverse but if epistemic privilege is not automatic then there must be some criteria by which we are claiming standpoints as legitimate or not, as meaningful contributors to research agendas or not, and that requires relating standpoints to some other metric, or, as Susan Hekman claims, to some "shared discourse" or "metanarrative" by which we can judge (1997, 355). This is critical in sorting out what exactly constitutes epistemic advantage. Are marginalized standpoints advantaged in virtue of critically conscious marginalized knowers recognizing our own epistemic authority or in virtue of those with social power choosing to confer epistemic advantage to the those who adequately occupy the relevant standpoint? If occupants of critical standpoints are determined to be epistemically advantaged due to *being conferred* so by dominant knowing and the dominant epistemic framework, then epistemic advantage is no better than any other form of epistemic charity. If standpoints are determined to be advantageous *internally,* or by marginalized social groups ourselves, then it is unclear why epistemic advantage would "contingently accrue" to a group, as Wylie argues, instead of applying by necessity. But, as they suggest, this is *clearly untenable.*

When Patricia Hill Collins writes that standpoint theory is not primarily a theory of truth and method but a theory of how systems of power impact knowledge production, she highlights an important tension within standpoint theory. "Standpoints may be judged not only by their epistemological contributions but also by the terms of their participation in hierarchical power relations," she argues, "Do they inherently explain and condone injustice, or do they challenge it? Do they participate in relations of rule via creating knowledge, or do they reject such rule by generating cultures of resistance?" (Collins 1997, 380). How can we avoid partial perspectives deciding the epistemic merits of other partial perspectives without invoking identity prejudicial social hierarchies? Standpoints and the epistemic advantages that they may or may not accrue puts the issue of truth in sharp relief but it also puts the issue of social power in sharp relief. Assessments of epistemic advantage often lie in the hands of those with social power and thus conferring epistemic advantage becomes another mechanism by which more dominantly situated knowers accept or reject marginalized standpoints and marginalized perspectives. Collins writes, "attempts to take the knowledge while leaving the power behind inadvertently operate within the terrain of privileged knowledge" (1997, 381). I take this to mean that dominant knowers ought not reap the benefits of marginalized standpoints and perspectives while leaving systems of social power that maintain marginalization and oppression happily in place.

Bat-Ami Bar On also argues that the concept of epistemic advantage functions as a way of marking relations of social power between marginalized groups—and thus distance from the center of power—and creates problems between socially marginalized groups. "The source of the problem," she writes, "is the existence of multiple socially marginalized groups; is any one of these groups more epistemically privileged than the others, and if that is not so—if they are all equally epistemically privileged—does epistemic privilege matter?" (Bar On 1993, 89). The problem with assignments of epistemic advantage based on marginalized identities is that both marginality and centrality, as the source of social power, are heterogenous. Thus assignments of privilege end up idealizing some social identities and some practices and excluding others (Bar On 1993, 92). Bar On argues that although this should compel theorists to abandon the concept of epistemic advantage, the concept also offers room for marginalized knowers to make claims of authority where we are typically denied it:

[T]he claim for epistemic privilege has served to empower movements of oppressed people in important ways. Taken quite generally, the claim of epistemic privilege in the realm of sociopolitical theory mostly justifies claims for authority, specifically the authority of members of socially marginalized groups to speak for themselves, which is an authority they do not have if everyone is equally capable to know them and their situation. Through this justification they grant themselves the authority to produce their own self-defined description of themselves and the world. And they demand that their voices, voices that have been excluded through the process of social marginalization, be given the respectful attention given to the voices of socioculturally hegemonic experts . . . Given this understanding of the strategic uses of the claim to epistemic privilege, it seems that what members of socially marginalized groups do by claiming epistemic privilege is to constitute themselves as socially differentiated, rather than individuated, Enlightenment subjects. (1993, 94–95)

Bar On argues, however, that epistemic advantage functions much like I describe epistemic charity. It is an assignment of epistemic authority but an assignment in absence of real social power. It is legitimated only by the willingness of dominant knowers to *listen*: "A socially marginalized group does not have the power to exclude, silence, and command obedience from a dominant group," Bar On argues, "its claims for epistemic privilege, lacking a social power on which to base them, cannot yield the same results as the self-authorizing claims of the dominant group and are, therefore, merely normative, compelling only for those who are theoretically persuaded by them" (1993, 96). If we are serious about marginalized knowing and the epistemic self-determination of marginalized knowers and marginalized groups, e.g., the ability to choose one's own epistemic projects, engage in one's own methods of justification, and engage in one's own knowledge-making practices without social and/or political threat, then *social power* is a necessary component. Social power is needed such that marginalized knowers are free to construct our own epistemic worlds and are not compelled to "world travel" out of necessity and survival, as María Lugones describes it, between worlds that are constructed by others and the worlds that we construct for ourselves (Lugones 1987, 11):

We and you do not talk the same language. When we talk to you we use your language: the language of your experiences and your theories. We try to use it to communicate our world of experience. But since your language and your theories are inadequate in expressing our experiences, we only succeed in communicating our experiences of exclusion. We cannot talk to you in our language because you do not understand it . . . we either use your language and distort our experience not just in the speaking about it, but in the living of it, or that we remain silent . . . we have had to be in your world and learn its ways. We have to participate in it, make a living in it, live in it, be mistreated in it, be ignored in it, and rarely, be appreciated in it. In learning to do these things or in learning to suffer them or in learning to enjoy what is to be enjoyed or in learning to understand your conception of us, we have had to learn your culture and thus your language and self-conceptions. But there is nothing that necessitates that you understand our world: understand, that is, not as an observer understands things, but as a participant, as *someone who has a stake* in them understands them. (Lugones and Spelman 1983, 575, my italics)

But what does it mean, as Lugones and Spelman claim, for dominant knowers to "have a stake" in marginalized knowing? As I suggest in the final section of this project, to have a stake in marginalized knowing means having an interest in finding ways to dismantle the hegemonic nature of dominant knowing. Epistemic justice, like social justice, is not a matter of individual will, or a matter of extensions of credibility or advantage to marginalized knowers on the part of dominant knowers. Epistemic justice involves dismantling the automatic epistemic privilege of *dominant knowing* and delegitimizing the social power that underwrites it. "The master's tools will never dismantle the master's house," Bar On argues, citing the famous quote by Audre Lorde, "although the claim to epistemic privilege as a tool may seem to be a claim of the oppressed, due to some of its history, it nonetheless reveals itself also a master's tool" (1993, 97). "There are no tools that can replace it, nor are any needed," she continues, "because when the oppressed feel a need to authorize speech, they are acting on feelings that are a function of their oppression. Speech needs to be authorized only where silence is the rule" (Bar On 1993, 97).

A strong interpretation of the inversion thesis acknowledges that the world could have been understood otherwise. This means that the type of epistemological practices that we now value might look very different in a world outside of the dominant framework. Part of thinking through the value of standpoints is to recognize that epistemic self-determination and the ability to make and understand the world as one sees fit is a critical part of being a human being. It is this ability that has been historically denied to marginalized groups. Granting that marginalized knowers may use our oppression as a critical key to unlock the epistemic projects of dominant groups, or to increase the objectivity in a world that we have not made, is a bitter reward for social and epistemic wrongs. Our present day epistemologies have arrived at their current state by way of a variety of interrelated historical, social, political, and epistemic injustices. Remediating those injustices demands more than epistemic charity and more than the sometimes conferred epistemic advantage suggested of marginalized standpoints. Theorizing marginalized knowing and realizing epistemic justice means prioritizing the voices of the oppressed on our own terms, and, in an important sense, in our own epistemic language. It is simply not enough to decide when and where marginalized knowers will be heard and when and where we can contribute to the epistemic projects of dominant others. Notice that I insist on separating concerns of truth from concerns of epistemic justice. This is not because I think that the two are not related but because it is still unclear *how* exactly situated knowledge theses are related to the truth-directedness of inquiry. However, I do not think that this means that we ought to deny the practical reality that knowledge is situated and that aspects of social situatedness like social power can corrupt our knowledge practices. I can only hope that remediating the social origins of our corrupted epistemic practices will have knock on effects in terms of truth and objectivity and, as with Harding's promise of "strong objectivity," will lead to better epistemic futures.

The recognition that social power is imperative for epistemic authority compels the conclusion that social power must be dispersed. When Lorde writes, "the master's tools will never dismantle the master's house," she is not suggesting that marginalized people abandon all claims to social power but instead that the "master's" conception of social power, and the mechanisms by which it was achieved, are faulty starting points to challenge that power. The master's tools are the ones that tell marginalized knowers that extensions of epistemic credibility or epistemic charity are sufficient to make us complete epistemic agents, self-authorizing in our own right. But such practices will never provide real social and epistemic justice or real social and epistemic liberation. Epistemic justice should predicated on the redistribution of social power and the ability to have our speech matter without *gifted* epistemic authority. The question is *how* can we achieve redistributions of social power in order to bring about real epistemic justice? I think it is helpful to look into the world for cases where marginalized groups are fighting for just such redistributions and to begin our analysis from those points. Consider the case of marginalized water activists in Flint, Michigan and Detroit, Michigan. Michael Doan theorizes these cases as critical and instructive examples of how structural epistemic injustice operates and how marginalized groups *make our meanings matter* within those unjust structures. These are not neat examples, or examples with clear resolutions, but they do illustrate how marginalized knowers might achieve epistemic justice by way of our own epistemic resources and bolstered by our own sense of epistemic authority.

Doan begins by examining the role of state-appointed emergency managers for cities in financial distress. Doan notes that the "stories a state legislature elects to tell itself" about financial distress directly shapes the "economic metrics and legal frameworks it ends up creating for enabling state interventions" (2017, 181). The ability to shape a story, or narrative, that impacts laws, policies, and procedures that in turn impact marginalized communities offers a clear example of epistemic power or epistemic authority. This epistemic power also allows dominant knowers, or knowers with social power, to silence or discredit narratives emerging from marginalized groups, as was seen in the case of the Flint Water Crisis:

"Flint residents had knowledge of the water crisis almost immediately upon the switch to the Flint River" (35). Why, then was their 'real and visceral' knowledge not taken up for months on end? Why have Flint residents not been taken seriously as knowers? Why has their knowledge not mattered to EMs, the Department of Treasury, the Department of Environmental Quality, or the Governor, whose inaction has prolonged and worsened the ongoing water crisis? And why have low-income, most African-American Detroiters been subjected to similar treatment while struggling to pay unaffordable water bills and facing shutoffs numbering in the tens of thousands? Why have the 'knowledge-&-power' matrices' of state officials been so resistant to change when 'challenged from below'? (Doan 2017, 178)

Doan argues that this is *epistemic redlining* or a form of epistemic injustice that cannot be linked to individual prejudice or resolved by the cultivation and application of epistemic virtue. Epistemic redlining gets its name from John McKnight's concept of redlining, or the systematic denial of goods and services to certain neighborhoods and communities due to race, ethnicity, poverty rates, etc., and not due to individual financial prospects or abilities. In cases of epistemic redlining, epistemic credibility is denied to residents of communities in financial distress or financial emergency. "What Michigan's EM law says," Doan argues, "is that *being in a state of financial emergency is a mark of a local population's inability to govern themselves*" (2017, 183). Notice that denying epistemic credibility on these grounds both precludes discussions of other *competing* factors of financial distress and effectively silences marginalized groups on what only appears to be the neutral grounds of fiscal health: Without explicitly naming people of color and the poor as "incapable of self-governance," emergency management uses the measure of fiscal health to exclude groups from "testifying and being heard on matters of public policy, not to mention from asking relevant questions, contesting claims and standards of evidence, and otherwise participating in inform-ing the policies that . . . shape their individual and collective lives" (Doan 2017, 183–184). Doan argues that epistemic redlining as a form of structural epistemic injustice cannot be tied to any individual perpetrator. Thus it will demand structural or institutional remediation.

Doan himself has been working with grassroots organizations in Michigan to repeal the laws that authorize emergency managers. In this sense, he is both part of what Nancy Arden McHugh calls a "community of epistemic resistance" and part of a community that is actively revealing how structural or institutional epistemic injustice operates. Following the work of Chandra Mohanty, José Medina and others, McHugh describes communities of epis-temic resistances as arising from resistance to dominant epistemologies, the examination of biases and prejudices, critically assessing ignorance and cognitive gaps, and developing epistemic virtues that allow for a "subversive lucidity" to emerge (2017, 537). This lucidity, McHugh claims, can feed epistemic agency. "An oppressed community develops into a community of epistemic resistance through the intentional development of a subversive lucidity that reformulates the epistemic terrain" (McHugh 2017, 538). Theorizing through the lens of her work with the London Correctional Institution's Wittenberg University Writing Group, McHugh describes working with incarcerated communities to form an "epistemology of incarceration," emphasizing that even in cases where some of the highest levels of testimonial injustice occur epistemic resistance can still be found: "When we acknowledge that marginalized communities resist epistemic injustice, we can recognize that although epistemic injustice *is* an injustice, it is not an epistemic dead end" (2017, 542). Communities of epistemic resistance may offer critical starting points for dominant social structures and social institutions committed to remedying epistemic injustice by presenting alternative epistemologies rooted in social and political struggle—epistemologies unsanctioned and unmediated by dominant knowing.

In Doan's case, he found that the personal stories of the water crisis emerging from communities in Detroit and Flint contributed to a "counternarrative" used by journalists, researchers, and those engaged in "citizen-led" policy creation and direct-action campaigns (2018). The community also worked with academic experts (in what I would call an *evolving epistemic community*) to expand and amplify their voices—"conforming to specific norms to secure recognition for particular purposes (e.g., working through established channels of expertise to force the state to publicly acknowledge the existence of lead and other forms of contamination)" (Doan 2018). Communities of epistemic resistance can reveal how institutional or structural epistemic injustice operates by creating and disseminating alternate epistemic resources and inverting dominant institutional understandings of social, political, and economic issues as in the counternarratives created about the water crises in Michigan. Following the work of Nancy Fraser, Doan calls these acts of epistemic resistance "transformative strategies" for addressing epistemic injustice in that they "aim to resist the reproduction of the social structures in question," contribute to the "radical restructuring" of those social structures, and "create new terms, values, and conditions by which people are to recognize one another as thinkers, knowers, and collaborators, contributing thereby to broader processes of social, economic, and political restructuring" (2018). Although communities of epistemic resistance can have internal epistemic goals, aimed at self-development or the psychic or material survival of the community itself, it is the outward facing epistemic acts of resistance that may best motivate changes in dominant social structures and institutions.

When dominant social structures and institutions have a stake in marginalized knowing and in further expanding the epistemic agency of marginalized groups, epistemic justice can both be *centered* on the perspectives of marginalized communities and *operationalized* as what Elizabeth Anderson refers to as a virtue of social institutions. Using McHugh's model of epistemic resistance and Doan's concept of a transformative strategy, we might go further by hypothesizing a *collaborative transformative strategy* where dominant social institutions with a stake, or vested interest, in marginalized knowing, utilize the perspectives of communities of epistemic resistance as source points for centered conceptions of structural epistemic justice. Thus marginalized knowers can take charge of a critical part of the solution or remedy for the rampant epistemic injustice that we encounter. This model inverts most remedies for epistemic injustice—remedies that stem from Miranda Fricker's initial agent-based analysis—and instead focuses on how dominant groups can socially and structurally aid in the expansion of marginalized perspectives and marginalized epistemic resources in ways that will radically outlast any particular testimonial encounter. This inversion retools the perverse idea that it is the role of individual dominant knowers to give or extend epistemic credibility according to their virtuous desires or as they see fit. As Doan writes:

> *Fricker's analysis of testimonial injustice focuses one-sidedly on the agency and prejudice of perpetrators, occluding the agency and resistance of victims.* Not only are the unjustly discredited, silenced, and excluded, given no role in initiating or guiding the work of correcting for testimonial injustice, but the question is left conspicuously unasked whether they might also take responsibility for demanding the recognition of their oppressors or find themselves moved to press for broader changes in their social and material conditions (rather than, say, going around trying to fix all the vicious hearers). In an odd twist, Fricker presents the perpetrators of testimonial injustice as the chief protagonists of change, driven to mend a damaged web of epistemic relations by their own desire to become more virtuous—or, at least, so we are invited to hope. Meanwhile, their victims are cast as the passive recipients of a form of epistemic recognition still to come and seemingly have nothing to do but wait patiently for their abusers to come around. (2018)

Consider how this might work using with Anderson's model of epistemic justice as a virtue of social structures and institutions. "It is not wrong to promote the practices of individual testimonial and hermeneutical injustice," she argues, "but in the face of massive structural injustice, *individual epistemic virtue plays a comparable role to the practice of individual charity in the context of massive structural poverty*" (Anderson 2012, 171, my italics). Anderson argues that we need to move beyond individual models of testimonial injustice and consider the socio-structural ways in which marginalized knowers are denied credibility. She identifies three primary structural causes of credibility deficits: "differential access to the markers of credibility; ethnocentrism; and the 'shared reality bias'" (Anderson 2012, 169). Markers of credibility include education and judgments of one's having had a "proper" education through metrics like using standardized grammar rules, ethnocentrism understood as in-group favoritism, and having a shared reality, or the "tendency of individuals who interact frequently to converge in their perspectives on and judgments about the world (Hardin and Conley 2001)" (Anderson 2012, 170). Anderson describes these features as mostly innocent features of our social world that result in structural disadvantages for marginalized groups. Theses structural disadvantages can, in turn, lead dominant groups to discredit or deflate the testimonies of socially marginalized groups. "From the perspective of the advantaged, what the disadvantaged are saying may make no sense," she argues, "because the interpretative resources they have developed to make sense of the experiences the advantaged share with one another are inadequate for comprehending the experiences of those from whom they are isolated" (Anderson 2012, 170). To this, she argues, the complaints of marginalized groups "may fall on deaf ears, not out of prejudice, but out of sheer incomprehension" (Anderson 2012, 170).

A critical part of the problem with addressing epistemic injustice lies in addressing the dominant frameworks that normalize and naturalize entire *ways of knowing*. This includes the uncritical acceptance of metrics of epistemic credibility including the use of standardized grammar and the reliance on *in-groupness* and having a shared reality. Aside from the fact that in-groupness and shared reality bias might *not* be cognitively innocent (see Chapter 1), much of what Anderson takes for granted in this discussion are the very epistemological assumptions that are at issue. Taking the dominant epistemic framework as the only framework that can confer epistemic credibility is problematic and leaves little to no room for discussions of how marginalized epistemic resources fit into remediation strategies for structural epistemic injustice. What does seem right about Anderson's analysis is the claim that structural remedies for epistemic injustice require changing social organization on the ground. The idea being that restructuring our social institutions to be more equitable will prevent the type of epistemic injustice that arises from unequal and/or segregated access to epistemic good and resources, e.g., education, social and epistemic siloing, etc. There is a similar analysis in Anderson's earlier work on racial justice where she argues that racial integration is a "good" motivated by the desire to rectify past historical wrongs of racial discrimination and racial segregation. When the task of racial integration is taken out of the hands of particular individuals and made a goal of the system itself, as in the case of affirmative action, we can achieve better and more inclusive results. The same holds true for *epistemic integration*. "If group segregation is the structural ground of the types of epistemic injustice discussed above" she argues, "then group integration is a structural remedy–a virtue of epistemic institutions" (2012, 171).

The goal of social institutional change should not only be a commitment to equality, or integration, but a commitment to *partiality* or the recognition that specific, targeted redress ought to be sought on the grounds of promoting epistemic equality and epistemic justice. Social institutions should privilege the epistemic resources and perspectives of communities of epistemic resistance with the added goal of challenging the dominant epistemic framework as the default framework of analysis. This will mean that the epistemic values and virtues necessary for epistemic justice are informed directly by marginalized and oppressed communities, or from the bottom-up, and not from the position of those who are already dominantly situated, or from the top-down. In this view, marginalized knowers will also have a wider range of social policies and epistemic practices to appeal to in cases of testimonial injustice and epistemic labor because we will be part of creating and implementing epistemic justice ourselves at the level of social institutions. We will also able to address issues of willful ignorance as clear failures to adopt and utilize marginalized epistemic resources on the part of social institutions and to track how marginalized epistemic resources are incorporated in the creation, organization, and operation of social institutional spaces. To get a sense of how this can work, consider the 2019 New York City Commission on Human Rights campaign on fighting anti-Black racism in the New York City. In 2018, the Commission received 584 race-based harassment and discrimination complaints, with a large number coming from New York City's Black communities. In response, the Commission launched the "While Black" campaign, with the goal of chronicling and intervening in the kinds of discrimination that Black New Yorkers face while doing everyday activities like walking, working, shopping, driving, bird-watching, and so on.

Notably, the campaign encouraged Black New Yorkers to submit their stories, affirming not only legal rights in the face of race-based discrimination but also the human right not to live day-to-day in racially hostile environments. The stories served as epistemic resources for the Commission to adopt strategies and mechanisms for remediation that put the perspectives of marginalized knowers front and center. For example, in an incident that also occurred in 2018, the high-end retail store, Prada, was found using racist window displays. The Prada window figurines looked like monkeys in Blackface, dark-skinned with bright red lips, echoing the highly controversial character, Little Black Sambo. The display prompted a swift public backlash. Although the Prada store received complaints about its racist imagery from both Black employees and Black patrons of the store, it failed to act until receiving press from the mainstream media and from Black politicians like New York

City councilman, Jumaane Williams. The media attention compelled the store to cover its windows and remove the figurines. Store employees and corporate management were compelled by the New York Commission on Human Rights to undergo racial equity training and to provide long-term reporting on the demographic makeup of its employees, all with the aim of promoting racial equity and ensuring "cultural competency and understanding of history" (Friedman 2020). Resolutions of this type present a new, and perhaps controversial, model for addressing testimonial injustice and willful ignorance at the level of institutions. While the company maintains that it meant no harm and was unaware of the racially insensitive nature of their advertising, the NYC Commission on Human Rights forced the company to focus on its own willful ignorance of symbols of racial oppression in order to promote cultural competency. This also included the mandatory hiring of a director-level diversity officer who will work in conjunction with the city agency to review Prada designs before they are advertised or sold in the United States (Friedman 2020).

A large part of initiatives of this type focus on the inclusion of marginalized perspectives and marginalized knowers at all levels of corporate infrastructure as well as calling on corporations to "do their homework" about historical, systemic oppression of marginalized groups. That is, they require social institutions steeped in the meaning-making practices of dominant knowing to both learn and incorporate marginalized epistemic resources, and not on a one-off basis, but as part of the day-to-day operations of the institution. We can see this same process at work through other organizing campaigns by communities of epistemic resistance, e.g., #GirlsLikeUs, #BlackLivesMatter, and #MeToo, as they chronicle and coalesce related social experiences into powerful narratives that can be taken up as part of justice-oriented agendas of social and political institutions. It is a targeted way in which communities of epistemic resistance can create public-facing epistemic resources that can be incorporated into the creation and maintenance of social institutions with the goal of promoting widescale epistemic justice. This includes utilizing the epistemic resources created by Black Lives Matter activists to address historical racism in federal housing policies, criminal justice reform, and reforms to policing and police budgets. I note these examples to emphasize the point that social media technologies make access to marginalized epistemic resources both robust and widely available, even considering the ever increasing half-life of public attention. Once these resources are suitably institutionalized, marginalized knowers may no longer need to depend on capturing public interest in order to achieve social and epistemic justice. As Janai Nelson of the NAACP Legal Defense and Education Fund notes: "Videos of Black and Brown Americans being harassed while going about their daily lives seem to have proliferated in recent years, but the painful truth is that the only new aspect of this phenomenon is the attention it's getting" (NYC Commission on Human Rights, "NYC Commission on Human Rights Launches New Campaign" 2019).

Social institutions may be able to achieve epistemic justice where individuals cannot by redistributing social power and epistemic power within institutions, e.g., through hiring and promoting a significant number of marginalized knowers, incorporating marginalized epistemic resources, instituting diverse management practices, and orienting institutional goals around social justice, etc., but the internal operation of social institutions will still depend on the daily practices and behaviors of dominant knowers in relation to marginalized knowers. What happens if and when the culture of social institutions turns reactionary? Dispersing social power and epistemic power is a tricky business. In the case of the NYC Commission of Human Right's "While Black" campaign, the threat of reactionary politics and reactionary policies still looms over how these policies will fare in the future. Thinking about epistemic justice as a virtue of our social institutions may help move the *practical arm* of epistemic justice in the right direction but it leaves open the question of how far institutional change can go without swinging backwards in the long term. Thinking institutionally moves discussions of epistemic injustice beyond mere theorizing. It challenges dominant knowers with an investment in epistemic justice to work toward greater inclusion of marginalized knowers and marginalized epistemic resources into social institutions without saying much about the psychology of dominance and resistance to culture change. Fundamental theorizing still needs to be done on the social construction of *dominant* identities, the shifting relations of dominance and marginalization, and critically, reactionary practices and policies that arise from even the *perception* of reductions in social and epistemic power. That is, we need to turn the lens toward understanding how identifying as socially dominant might unjustly impact, and *inflate*, assessments of epistemic credibility and epistemic authority.

For example, consider how an uncritical acceptance of social dominance lies at the center of Fricker's analysis of the harm of testimonial injustice. She argues that, at the extreme end of epistemic objectification, persistent and systematic testimonial injustice harms marginalized knowers in fundamental capacities of what it means to be a human being, in our capacity to be knowers. "Persistent testimonial injustice can indeed inhibit the very formation of self," Fricker claims, operating such that a marginalized knower's own notion of self can be subsumed by the negative stereotypes operating upon them (2007, 55). The real power of identity power, she insists, is "identity power's ability to shape the people it cramps" (Fricker 2007, 56). Fricker does not question the power of dominant knowers to take away the very humanity of marginalized knowers. She does not question either the existence or the *rightness* of that power and, as such, reifies it for the very groups that desperately need to question it. The humanity of marginalized knowers is not tied to our recognition by the dominant powers that unjustly confer or withdraw epistemic credibility. That is indeed a perverse logic –but it is also a *revealing* logic. As Doan argues, and as I myself have argued in terms of epistemic labor, marginalized knowers are in dependent *relations of power* with dominant knowers. This relationship is epistemic in a way that might best be understood as trivial. Marginalized knowers recognize the power of dominant knowers to confer credibility because dominant knowers often control access to the material goods and resources that marginalized knowers need, e.g., safe drinking water, employment, bodily safety (Doan 2018). Conceiving of these relations of power in purely epistemic terms masks the role of dominant social power and thus masks a critical part of analyzing epistemic injustice.

As a final thought, I think that centering epistemic injustice is only part of the necessary prescription for understanding the multidimensionality of epistemic injustice. Like current calls to understand and unpack "whiteness" in order to do the hard work of dismantling white supremacy, dominantly situated knowers need to unpack the social origins of dominance and the multitude of mechanisms that allow for the features of social dominance to remain neatly tucked away, particularly as those features pertain to the creation and maintenance of social marginalization. I think that the key to long-lasting structural epistemic justice lies in analyses of this variety, as I have suggested throughout this project, the good will of dominant knowers, and their ability to have, and maintain, a stake in marginalized knowing goes only so far. At some point, dominant knowers must come face-to-face with the realities of the construction of their own social identities, including its contingency and artificiality. At the beginning of *The Souls of Black Folk,* when W. E. B. Du Bois considers the question of how it feels to be Black and thus a *problem* in the eyes of white America, the lens of analysis is pointed at a self that is bifurcated, created by the images of dominant others and by one's own history and community. As much as Black Americans are compelled toward double-consciousness, white Americans are compelled toward a single, unified consciousness, a consciousness that does not see itself clearly. This may be the most intractable problem facing epistemic justice. There is no corollary of Du Bois's question for those who are dominantly situated but it is question that still needs to be asked. Dismantling dominant knowing in the pursuit of epistemic justice may begin as easily as a look in the mirror, reframing the object of analysis, where dominant knowers ask themselves, in earnest: *How does it feel to be a problem?*

Bibliography

Alcoff, Linda Martín. 2010. "Epistemic Identities," *Episteme* 7(2):128–137.

Alcoff, Linda Martín. 2006. *Visible Identities: Race, Gender, and the Self.* Oxford: Oxford University Press.

Alcoff, Linda Martín. 1991. "The Problem of Speaking for Others." *Cultural Critique* 20 (Winter 1991–1992): 5–32.

Alcoff, Linda. 1988. "Cultural Feminism Versus Post-Structuralism: The Identity Crisis in Feminist Theory." *Signs: Journal of Women in Culture and Society* 13(3): 405–406.

Alexander, Ayanna. 2018. "African-Americans Feel Left Out of the Gun Debate." *Politico,* April 23. https://www.politico.com/magazine/story/2018/04/23/african-americans-feel-left-out-of-the-gun-debate-218068/.

Allen W. Johnson and Timothy Earle. 2000. *The Evolution of Human Societies: From Foraging Group to Agrarian State.* Stanford: Stanford University Press.

Amodio, David M., Patricia G. Devine, and Eddie Harmon-Jones. 2007. "A Dynamic Model of Guilt: Implications for Motivation and Self-Regulation in the Context of Prejudice." *Psychological Science* 18(6): 524–530.

Anderson, Elizabeth. 2012. "Epistemic Justice as a Virtue of Social Institutions." *Social Epistemology* 26(2): 163–173.

Anderson, Elizabeth. 2004. "Racial Integration as a Compelling Interest." *Constitutional Commentary* 21(1): 15–40.

Armstrong, Ken and T. Christian Miller. 2017. "When Sexual Assault Victims Are Charged With Lying." *The New York Times,* November 24. https://www.nytimes.com/2017/11/24/opinion/sunday/sexual-assault-victims-lying.html.

Baldwin, James. 1993. *The Fire Next Time.* New York: Vintage International.

Bar On, Bat-Ami. 1993. "Marginality and Epistemic Privilege." In *Feminist Epistemologies,* edited by Linda Alcoff and Elizabeth Potter, 94-96. New York, NY: Routledge.

Berenstain, Nora. 2020. "White Feminist Gaslighting." *Hypatia: A Journal of Feminist Philosophy* 35(4): 733–758.

Berenstain, Nora. 2016. "Epistemic Exploitation." *Ergo: An Open Access Journal of Philosophy* 3(22): 569–590.

Blair, Irene V., Jennifer E. Ma, and Alison P. Lenton. 2001. "Imagining Stereotypes Away: The Moderation of Implicit Stereotypes Through Mental Imagery." *Journal of Personality and Social Psychology* 81(5): 828–841.

Bratter, Jenifer L., Kristie J. Rowley, and Irina Chukhray. 2016. "Does a Self-Affirmation Intervention Reduce Stereotype Threat in Black and Hispanic High Schools?" *Race and Social Problems* 8(4): 340–356.

Brendl, Miguel C., Arthur B. Markman, and Claude Messner. 2001. "How Do Indirect Measures of Evaluation Work? Evaluating the Inference of Prejudice in the Implicit Association Test." *Journal of Personality and Social Psychology* 81(5): 760–773.

Bronner, Sasha and Emma Gray. 2015. "Patricia Arquette Causes Controversy Telling 'Gay People and People of Color' to Fight for Women's Rights." *HuffPost*, February 23. https://www.huffpost.com/entry/ patricia-arquette-controversy-people-of-color-gay-people_n_6734076.

Brown-Dean, Khalilah. 2019. *Identity Politics in the United States.* Cambridge: Polity Press.

Brownmiller, Susan and Dolores Alexander. 1992. "How We Got Here: From Carmita Wood to Anita Hill." *Ms. Magazine,* January/February 1992. http://www. nfwfwf.org/wp-content/uploads/2018/02/BROWNMILLER-ALEXANDER-MS-MAG-1992.pdf.

Burge, Tyler. 1993. "Content Preservation." *Philosophical Review* 102: 457–488.

Christensen, David. 2007. "Epistemology of Disagreement: The Good News." *Philosophical Review* 116: 187–217.

Code, Lorraine. 2014. "Feminist Epistemology and the Politics of Knowledge: Questions of Marginality." In *The SAGE Handbook of Feminist Theory,* edited by Mary Evans, Clare Hemmings, Marsha Henry, Hazel Johnstone, Sumi Madhok, Ania Plomien, and Sadie Wearing, 20–21. London: Sage Publications.

Code, Lorraine. 2007. "The Power of Ignorance." In *Race and Epistemologies of Ignorance* edited by Shannon Sullivan and Nancy Tuana, 213–230. Albany: State University of New York Press.

Code, Lorraine. 2006. *Ecological Thinking: The Politics of Epistemic Location.* Oxford: Oxford University Press.

Code, Lorraine. 1993. "Taking Subjectivity Into Account." In *Feminist Epistemologies* edited by Linda Alcoff and Elizabeth Potter, 15–48. New York: Routledge.

Code, Lorraine. 1987. *Epistemic Responsibility.* Hanover: University Press of New England.

Cohen, Geoffrey L. and David K. Sherman. 2014. "The Psychology of Change: Self-Affirmation and Social Psychological Intervention." *Annual Review of Psychology* 65: 333–371.

Collins, Patricia Hill. 2000. *Black Feminist Thought: Knowledge, Consciousness, and the Politics of Empowerment.* New York: Routledge.

Collins, Patricia Hill. 1999. "Reflections on the Outsider Within." *Journal of Career Development* 26(1): 85–88.

Collins, Patricia Hill. 1997. "Comment on Hekman's 'Truth and Method: Feminist Standpoint Theory Revisited': Where's the Power?" *Sign: Journal of Women in Culture and Society,* 22(2): 375–381.

Collins, Patricia Hill. 1986. "Learning From the Outsider Within: The Sociological Significance of Black Feminist Thought." *Social Problems* 33(6): 14–32.

Cone, Jeremy and Melissa J. Ferguson. 2015. "He Did What? The Role of Diagnosticity in Revising Implicit Evaluations." *Journal of Personality and Social Psychology* 108: 37–57.

Cooper, Brittney. 2015. "Black America's Hidden Tax: Why This Feminist of Color Is Going on Strike." *Salon,* February 25. http://www.salon.com/2015/02/25/black_americas_hidden_tax_why_this_feminist_of_color_is_going_on_strike/.

Correll, Joshua, Bernadette Park, Bernd Wittenbrink, and Charles M. Judd. 2002. "The Police Officer's Dilemma: Using Ethnicity to Disambiguate Potentially Threatening Individuals." *Journal of Personality and Social Psychology* 83(6): 1314–1329.

Crenshaw, Kimberle. 1989. "Demarginalizing the Intersection of Race and Sex: A Black Feminist Critique of Antidiscrimination Doctrine, Feminist Theory and Antiracist Politics." *University of Chicago Legal Forum* 1(8): 139–167.

Daniell, F. Raymond. 1937. "Weems Case Given to Alabama Jury." *The New York Times,* July 24. https://www.nytimes.com/1937/07/24/archives/weems-case-given-to-alabama-jury-another-scottsboro-trial-ends.html

Davidson, Lacey. 2019. "When Testimony Isn't Enough: Implicit Bias Research as Epistemic Exclusion." In *Overcoming Epistemic Injustice,* edited by Benjamin Sherman and Stacey Goguen, 269–284. Lanham: Rowman and Littlefield.

De Dreu, C.K.W., Shaul Shalvi, Lindred L. Greer, Gerben A. Van Kleef, and Michel J. J. Handgraaf. 2012. "Oxytocin Motivates Non-Cooperation In Intergroup Conflict To Protect Vulnerable In-Group Members." *PLoS One* 7(11): e46751.

De Dreu, Carsten K. W., Lindred L. Greer, Gerben A. Van Kleef, Shaul Shalvi, and Michel J. J. Handgraaf. 2011. "Oxytocin Promotes Human Ethnocentrism." *Proceedings of the National Academy of Sciences USA* 108: 1262–1266.

De Sousa Santos, Boaventura. 2016. *Epistemologies of the South: Justice Against Epistemicide.* New York: Routledge.

Devine, Patricia G. and Margo J. Monteith. 1993. "The Role of Discrepancy-Associated Affect in Prejudice Reduction." In *Affect, Cognition and Stereotyping: Interactive Processes in Group Perception,* edited by Diane M. Mackie and David L. Hamilton, 317–344. San Diego: Academic Press.

DiAngelo, Robin. 2018. *White Fragility: Why It's So Hard to Talk to White People About Racism.* Boston: Beacon Press.

DiAngelo, Robin. 2011. "White Fragility." *International Journal of Critical Pedagogy* 3(3): 54–70.

Doan, Michael. 2018. "Resisting Structural Epistemic Injustice." *Feminist Philosophy Quarterly* 4(4). https://doi.org/10.5206/fpq/2018.4.6230.

Doan, Michael P. 2017. "Epistemic Injustice and Epistemic Redlining." *Ethics and Social Welfare* 11(2): 177–190.

Dotson, Kristie. 2014a. "Thinking Familiar with the Interstitial: An Introduction." *Hypatia: A Journal of Feminist Philosophy,* Special Issue: *Interstices: Inheriting Women of Color Feminist Philosophy* 29(1): 1–17.

Dotson, Kristie. 2014b. "Conceptualizing Epistemic Oppression." *Social Epistemology: A Journal of Knowledge, Culture and Policy* 28(2): 17–18.

Dotson, Kristie. 2012. "A Cautionary Tale: On Limited Epistemic Oppression." *Frontiers: A Journal of Women Studies* 33(1): 24–47.

Dotson, Kristie. 2011. "Tracking Epistemic Violence, Tracking Practices of Silencing." *Hypatia: A Journal of Feminist Philosophy* 26(2): 236–257.

Du Bois, W. E. B. 1903. *The Souls of Black Folk.* Reprint of the 1903 Chicago Edition, Project Gutenberg, 2008. https://www.gutenberg.org/files/408/408-h/408-h.htm.

Elga, Adam. 2007. "Reflection and Disagreement." *Noûs* 41(3): 478–502.

Elga, Adam. 2005. "On Overrating Oneself . . . And Knowing It." *Philosophical Studies* 123 (1–2): 115–124.

Fanon, Frantz. 1986. *Black Skin, White Masks.* London: Pluto Press.

Fazio, Russell H. and Michael A. Olson. 2003. "Implicit Measures in Social Cognition Research: Their Meaning and Uses." *Annual Review of Psychology* 54(1): 297–327.

Fielder, Klaus, Claude Messner, and Matthias Bluemke. 2006. "Unresolved Problems With the 'I,' the 'A,' and the 'T': A Logical and Psychometric Critique of the Implicit Association Test (IAT)." *European Review of Social Psychology* 17(1): 74–147.

Forscher, Patrick S., Calvin K. Lai, Jordan R. Axt, Charles R. Ebersole, Michelle Herman, Patricia G. Devine, and Brian A. Nosek. 2018. "A Meta-Analysis of Procedures to Change Implicit Measures." [Preprint]. https://doi.org/10.31234/osf.io/dv8tu.

Foucault, Michel. 1982. "The Subject and Power." *Critical Inquiry* 8(4): 777–795.

Frances, Bryan. (2012). "Discovering Disagreeing Epistemic Peers and Superiors." *International Journal of Philosophical Studies* 20(1): 1–21.

Fricker, Miranda. 2013. "How Is Hermeneutical Injustice Related to 'White Ignorance'?" *Social Epistemology Review and Reply Collective* 2(8): 49–53.

Fricker, Miranda. 2010. "Replies to Alcoff, Goldberg, and Hookway on Epistemic Injustice." *Episteme* 7(2): 164–178.

Fricker, Miranda. 2007. *Epistemic Injustice: Power and the Ethics of Knowing.* Oxford: Oxford University Press.

Fricker, Miranda. 2006. "Powerlessness and Social Interpretation." *Episteme: A Journal of Social Epistemology* 3(1–2): 96–108.

Friedman, Vanessa. 2020. "Miuccia Prada Will Be Getting Sensitivity Training." *The New York Times,* February 4. https://www.nytimes.com/2020/02/04/style/Prada-racism-City-Commission-on-Human-Rights.html.

Gandbhir, Geeta and Blair Foster. 2015. "A Conversation With My Black Son." *The New York Times,* March 17. https://www.nytimes.com/2015/03/17/opinion/a-conversation-with-my-black-son.html.

Gandhi, Neha. 2019. "Gloria Steinem: Don't Forget We Have a Harasser in the White House." *Girlboss*, March 25. https://www.girlboss.com/read/gloria-steinem-interview-sexual-harassment-feminism-trump.

Gay, Roxane. 2018. "Lots of People Love, 'To Kill a Mockingbird.' Roxane Gay Isn't One of Them." *The New York Times,* June 18. https://www.nytimes.com/2018/06/18/books/review/tom-santopietro-why-to-kill-a-mockingbird-matters.html.

Gendler, Tamar Szabó. 2011. "On The Epistemic Costs of Implicit Bias." *Philosophical Studies* 156 (1):33–63.

Glaberson, William. 2013. "Faltering Courts, Mired in Delays." *The New York Times,* April 13. https://www.nytimes.com/2013/04/14/nyregion/justice-denied-bronx-court-system-mired-in-delays.html.

Glaser, Jack and Eric D. Knowles. 2008. "Implicit Motivation to Control Prejudice." *Journal of Experimental Social Psychology* 44 (1): 164–172.

Glick, Peter. 1991. "Trait-Based and Sex-Based Discrimination in Occupational Prestige, Occupational Salary, and Hiring." *Sex Roles* 25: 351-378.

Goldman, Alvin. 1999. *Knowledge in a Social World.* Oxford: Oxford University Press.

Gonnerman, Jennifer. 2014. "Before the Law." *The New Yorker,* September 29. https://www.newyorker.com/magazine/2014/10/06/before-the-law.

Green, Nadege. 2018. "In Parkland, Shutting Down a Black Lives Matter Statement Days Before Shooting." *WLRN Public Media,* April 6. http://www.wlrn.org/post/parkland-shutting-down-black-lives-matter-statement-days-shooting.

Greenwald, Anthony G., Banaji R. Mahzarin, and Brian A. Nosek. 2015. "Statistically Small Effects of the Implicit Association Test Can Have Societally Large Effects." *Journal of Personality and Social Psychology* 108 (4): 553–561.

Hamilton, David L. and Robert K. Gifford. 1976. "Illusory Correlation in Interpersonal Perception: A Cognitive Bias of Stereotypic Judgments." *Journal of Experimental Social Psychology* 12 (4): 392–407.

Hardin, Curtis and Terri Conley. 2001. "A Relational Approach to Cognition: Shared Experience and Relationship Affirmation in Social Cognition." In *Cognitive Social Psychology: The Princeton Symposium on the Legacy and Future of Social Cognition* edited by Gordon Moskowitz, 3–17. Mahwah, New Jersey: Erlbaum.

Harding, Sandra and Kathryn Norberg. 2005. "New Feminist Approaches to Social Science Methodologies: An Introduction." *Signs: Journal of Women in Culture and Society* 30 (4): 2009–2015.

Harding, Sandra. 1995. "'Strong Objectivity': A Response to the New Objectivity Question." *Synthese* 104 (3): 331–349.

Harding, Sandra. 1993. "Rethinking Standpoint Epistemology: What Is 'Strong Objectivity.'" In *Feminist Epistemologies,* edited by Linda Alcoff and Elizabeth Potter, 49–82. New York: Routledge.

Harding, Sandra. 1991. *Whose Science? Whose Knowledge? Thinking from Women's Lives.* Ithaca: Cornell University Press.

Harris, Aisha. 2018. "When Black Performers Use Their 'White Voice.'" *The New York Times,* July 10. https://www.nytimes.com/2018/07/10/movies/when-black-performers-use-their-white-voice.html.

Hekman, Susan. 1997. "Truth and Method: Feminist Standpoint Theory Revisited." *Signs: Journal of Women in Culture and Society* 22 (2): 341–365.

Jenkins, Melissa A., Philip J. Langlais, Dean Delis, and Ronald Cohen. 1998. "Learning and Memory in Rape Victims With Posttraumatic Stress Disorder." *The American Journal of Psychiatry* 155 (2): 278–279.

Jorgensen, Jillian. 2017. "Mayoral Candidate Akeem Browder Addresses Past as Registered Sex Offender, Convicted Felon." *The Daily News,* June 26. http://www.nydailynews.com/news/politics/ mayoral-candidate-akeem-browder-talks-sex-offender-felon-article-1.3279786.

Kawakami, Kerry, John F. Dovidio, and Simone van Kamp. 2005. "Kicking the Habit: Effects of Nonstereotypic Association Training and Correction Processes on Hiring Decisions." *Journal of Experimental Social Psychology* 41 (1): 68–75.

Kawakami, Kerry, John F. Dovidio, Jasper F. Moll, J. F., Sander Hermsen, and Abby Russin. 2000. "Just Say No (To Stereotyping): Effects Of Training in Negation of Stereotypic Associations on Stereotype Activation." *Journal of Personality and Social Psychology* 78 (5): 871–888.

Kees Keizer, Siegwart Lindenberg, and Linda Steg. 2008. "The Spreading of Disorder." *Science* 322 (5908): 1681–1685.

Kelkar, Kamala. 2018. "Parkland, Race, and the Gun Violence That Goes Overlooked." *PBS News Hours,* March 18. https://www.pbs.org/newshour/nation/ parkland-race-and-the-gun-violence-that-goes-overlooked.

Khan-Cullors, Patrisse and Asha Bandele. 2017. *When They Call You a Terrorist: A Black Lives Matter Memoir.* New York: St. Martin's Griffin.

Klarman, Michael J. 2009. "Scottsboro." *Marquette Law Review* 93: 379–431.

Klarman, Michael J. 2000. "The Racial Origins of Modern Criminal Procedure." *Michigan Law Review* 99 (1): 48–97.

Lackey, Jennifer. 2006. "Knowing From Testimony." *Philosophy Compass* 1(5): 432–448.

Landman, Tanya. 2015. "Is To Kill a Mockingbird a Racist Book?" *The Guardian,* October 20. https://www.theguardian.com/childrens-books-site/2015/oct/20/ is-to-kill-a-mockingbird-a-racist-book-tanya-landman.

Lockhart, P. R. 2018. "Parkland Is Sparking a Difficult Conversation About Race, Trauma, and Public Support." *Vox,* February 24. https://www.vox.com/identities/2018/2/24/17044904/ parkland-shooting-race-trauma-movement-for-black-lives-gun-violence.

Longino, Helen E. 1999. "Feminist Epistemology." In *The Blackwell Guide to Epistemology*, edited by John Grecco and Ernest Sosa, 327–353. Malden: Blackwell Publishing.

Longino, Helen E. 1993. "Feminist Standpoint Theory and the Problems of Knowledge." *Signs: Journal of Women and Culture in Society* 19(1): 201–212.

Longino, Helen E. 1993. "Subjects, Power, and Knowledge: Description and Prescription in Feminist Philosophies of Science." In *Feminist Epistemologies,* edited by Elizabeth Potter and Linda Alcoff, 101–120. New York: Routledge.

Lorde, Audre and Roxane, Gay. 2020. *The Selected Works of Audre Lorde.* [Google eBook Edition]. New York: W. W. Norton and Company.

Lugones, María. 1987. "Playfulness, 'World'-Travelling, and Loving Perception." *Hypatia: A Journal of Feminist Philosophy* 2(2): 3–19.

Lugones, María C. and Elizabeth V. Spelman. 1983. "Have We Got a Theory for You! Feminist Theory, Cultural Imperialism, and the Demand for 'The Women's Voice.'" *Women's Studies International Forum* 6 (6): 575–576.

Mason, Rebecca. 2011. "Two Kinds of Unknowing." *Hypatia: A Journal of Feminist Philosophy* 26(2): 294–307.

McHugh, Nancy Arden. 2017. "Epistemic Communities and Institutions." In *The Routledge Handbook of Epistemic Injustice* edited by Ian James Kidd, José Medina, and Gaile Pohlhaus Jr. [Google eBook Edition]. New York: Routledge. https://play. google.com/books/reader?id=ctORDgAAQBAJ&pg=GBS.RA1-PT293.

McKinney, Rachel. 2016. "Extracted Speech." *Social Theory and Practice* 42 (2): 258–284.

McKinnon, Rachel. 2017. "Allies Behaving Badly: Gaslighting as Epistemic Injustice." In *The* Routledge Handbook of Epistemic Injustice edited by Ian James Kidd, José Medina, and Gaile Pohlhaus Jr. [Google eBook Edition]. New York: Routledge. https://play.google.com/books/reader?id=ctORDgAAQBAJ&pg=GBS. RA1-PT293.

Medina, José. 2013. *The Epistemology of Resistance: Gender and Racial Oppression, Epistemic Injustice, and Resistant Imaginations.* Oxford: Oxford University Press.

Medina, José. 2012. "Hermeneutical Injustice and Polyphonic Contextualism: Social Silences and Shared Hermeneutical Responsibilities." *Social Epistemology* 26(2): 201–220.

Mendoza, Saaid, Peter Gollwitzer, and David Amodio. 2010. "Reducing the Expression of Implicit Stereotypes: Reflexive Control through Implementation Intentions." *Personality and Social Psychology Bulletin* 36(4): 512–523.

Miller, Hayley. 2018. "Parkland Survivors Call Out Media For Ignoring Gun Violence in Black Communities." *HuffPost,* March 19. https://www.huffingtonpost.com/ entry/parkland-gun-violence-black-communities_us_5ab00986e4b0e862383a68f9.

Miller, T. Christian and Ken Armstrong. 2015. "An Unbelievable Story of Rape." *ProPublica* and *The Marshall Project,* December 16. https://www.propublica.org/ article/false-rape-accusations-an-unbelievable-story.

Mills, Charles. 2013. "White Ignorance and Hermeneutical Injustice: A Comment on Medina and Fricker." *Social Epistemology Review and Reply Collective* 3 (1): 38–43.

Mills, Charles. 2007. "White Ignorance." In *Race and Epistemologies of Ignorance,* edited by Shannon Sullivan and Nancy Tuana, 13–38. Albany: State University of New York Press.

Mills, Charles. 1998. *Blackness Visible: Essays on Philosophy and Race.* Ithaca: Cornell University Press.

Mills, Charles. 1997. *The Racial Contract.* Ithaca: Cornell University Press.

Monteith, Margo. 1993. "Self-Regulation of Prejudiced Responses: Implications for Progress in Prejudice-Reduction Efforts." *Journal of Personality and Social Psychology* 65(3): 469–485.

Moskowitz, Gordon and Li, Peizhong. 2011. "Egalitarian Goals Trigger Stereotype Inhibition." *Journal of Experimental Social Psychology* 47(1): 103–116.

Moya, Paula. 2011. "Who We Are and From Where We Speak." *Transmodernity: Journal of Peripheral Cultural Production of the Luso-Hispanic World* 1(2): 79–94.

Moya, Paula M. L. and Michael R. Hames-García. 2000. *Reclaiming Identity: Realist Theory and the Predicament of Postmodernism.* Berkeley: University of California Press.

Murphy, Robin A., Stefanie Schmeer, Frédéric Vallée-Tourangeau, Esther Mondragon, Denis Hilton. 2011. "Making the Illusory Correlation Effect Appear and then Disappear: The Effects of Increased Learning." *Quarterly Journal of Experimental Psychology* 64: 24-40.

New York City Commission on Human Rights. 2019. "While Black in NYC: Protections Against Discrimination for Black New Yorkers." New York: NYC Human Rights, 2019. https://www1.nyc.gov/site/cchr/media/while-black-nyc.page%20.

New York City Commission on Human Rights. 2019. "NYC Commission on Human Rights Launches New Campaign to Combat Anti-Black Racism in NYC." Press Release, March 15. https://www1.nyc.gov/assets/cchr/downloads/pdf/press-releases/While_Black_Campaign_Press_Release.pdf.

Nosek, Brian A., Anthony G. Greenwald and Mahzarin R. Banaji. 2007. "The Implicit Association Test At Age 7: A Methodological and Conceptual Review." In *Automatic Processes In Social Thinking and Behavior* edited by John A. Bargh, 265–292. New York: Psychology Press.

Oluo, Ijeoma. 2019. *So You Want to Talk About Race.* New York: Seal Press.

Oswald, Frederick L., Gregory Mitchell, Hart Blanton, James Jaccard, and Philip E. Tetlock. 2015. "Using the IAT to Predict Ethnic and Racial Discrimination: Small Effect Sizes of Unknown Societal Significance." *Journal of Personality and Social Psychology* 108 (4): 562–571.

Oswald, Frederick L., Gregory Mitchell, Hart Blanton, James Jaccard, and Philip E. Tetlock. 2013. "Predicting Ethnic and Racial Discrimination: A Meta-Analysis of IAT Criterion Studies." *Journal of Personality and Social Psychology* 105 (2): 171–192.

Park, Sang Hee, Jack Glaser, and Eric D. Knowles. 2008. "Implicit Motivation to Control Prejudice Moderates the Effect of Cognitive Depletion on Unintended Discrimination." *Social Cognition* 26 (4): 401–419.

Peirce, Charles Sanders. 2011. "The Fixation of Belief." In *Philosophical Writings of Peirce,* edited by Justus Buchler, 5–22. New York: Dover Publication.

Pitts, Byron, Katie Yu and Lauren Effron. 2015. "Who Kalief Browder Might Have Been If He Hadn't Spent Over 1,000 Days in Jail Without a Conviction." *ABCNews,* June 17. https://abcnews.go.com/US/kalief-browder-spent-1000-days-jail-charges/story?id=31832313.

Pohlhaus, Jr., Gaile. 2012. "Relational Knowing and Epistemic Injustice: Toward a Theory of Willful Hermeneutical Ignorance." *Hypatia: A Journal of Feminist Philosophy* 27(4): 715–735.

Posey, Kamili. 2021. "Epistemic Ignorance, Epistemic Distortion, and Narrative History 'Thick' and 'Thin.'" In *Lorraine Code: Thinking Responsibly, Thinking Ecologically,* edited by Nancy Arden McHugh and Andrea Doucet, forthcoming. Albany: SUNY Press.

Rokeach, Milton. 1973. *The Nature of Human Values.* New York: Free Press.

Rolin, Kristina. 2006. "The Bias Paradox in Standpoint Epistemology." *Episteme: A Journal of Individual and Social Epistemology* 3 (1–2): 125–136.

Rudman, Laurie A. and Peter Glick. 1999. "Feminized Management and Backlash Toward Agentic Women: The Hidden Costs to Women of a Kinder, Gentler, Image of Middle Management." *Journal of Personality and Social Psychology* 77: 1004-1010.

Sapolsky, Robert. 2017. *Behave: The Biology of Humans at Our Best and Worst.* New York: Penguin Books.

Saul, Jennifer. 2017. "Implicit Bias, Stereotype Threat, and Epistemic Injustice." In *The Routledge Handbook of Epistemic Injustice* edited by Ian James Kidd, José Medina, and Gaile Pohlhaus, Jr. [Google eBook Edition]. New York: Routledge. https://play.google.com/books/reader?id=ctORDgAAQBAJ&pg=GBS. RA1-PT293.

Schmid, Petra C. and David M. Amodio. 2017. "Power Effects on Implicit Prejudice and Stereotyping: The Role of Intergroup Face Processing." *Social Neuroscience* 12(2): 218–231.

Scott, Shirley J. 1963. "The Negro Walks on Eggshells." *The Ithaca Journal,* December 3. Page 7.

Seattle Channel. 2018. "Dr. Robin DiAngelo Discusses 'White Fragility.'" YouTube 1:23:30, July 3. https://www.youtube.com/watch?v=45ey4jgoxeU&t=3225s.

Spiers, Hugo. J., Bradley C. Love, Mike E. Le Pelley, Charlotte E. Gibb, and Robin A. Murphy. 2016. "Anterior Temporal Lobe Tracks the Formation of Prejudice." *Journal of Cognitive Neuroscience* 29 (3): 1–15. doi:10.1162/jocn_a_01056.

Spivak, Gayatri. 1988. "Can the Subaltern Speak?" In *Marxism and Interpretation of Culture,* edited by Cary Nelson and Lawrence Grossberg, 271–313. Urbana: University of Illinois Press.

St. Félix, Doreen. 2018. "The Twisted Power of White Voice in 'Sorry to Bother You' and 'Blackkklasman.'" *The New Yorker,* August 13. https://www.newyorker.com/culture/cultural-comment/ the-twisted-power-of-white-voice-in-sorry-to-bother-you-and-blackkklansman.

Steele, Claude M. and Thomas J. Liu. 1983. "Dissonance Processes as Self-Affirmation." *Journal of Personality and Social Psychology* 45 (1): 5–19.

Strebeigh, Fred. 2009. *Equal: Women Reshape American Law.* New York: W.W. Norton and Company.

Ten Velden, Femke S., Matthijs Baas, Shaul Shalvi, Mariska E. Kret, and Carsten K. W. De Dreu. 2014. "Oxytocin Differentially Modulates Compromise and Competitive Approach but Not Withdrawal to Antagonists From Own vs. Rivaling Other Groups." *Brain Research* 1580: 172–179.

Thompson, Questlove Ahmir. 2013. "Questlove: Trayvon Martin and I Ain't Shit." *New York Magazine,* July 16. http://nymag.com/daily/intelligencer/2013/07/questlove-trayvon-martin-and-i-aint-shit.html.

Thorsen, Karen, William Miles, Douglas K. Dempsey, Don Lenzer, Steven Olswang, Amiri Baraka, Ishmael Reed, William Styron, and Maya Angelou. 1989. *James Baldwin: The Price of the Ticket.* PBS/American Masters. http://digital.films.com/PortalPlaylists.aspx?aid=13753&xtid=49726.

Webb, Thomas L., Paschal Sheeran, and John Pepper. 2012. "Gaining Control Over Responses to Implicit Attitude Tests: Implementation Intentions Engender Fast Responses on Attitude-Incongruent Trials." *British Journal of Social Psychology* 51: 13–32.

Weekes Schroer, Jeanine. 2015. "Giving Them Something They Can Feel: On the Strategy of Scientizing the Phenomenology of Race and Racism." *Knowledge Cultures* 3 (1): 1–10.

Williams, Michael. 2001. "Contextualism, Externalism and Epistemic Standards." *Philosophical Studies: An International Journal for Philosophy in the Analytic Tradition* 103 (1): 1–23.

Williams, Patricia. 1991. *The Alchemy of Race and Rights: Diary of a Law Professor.* Cambridge: Harvard University Press.

Witt, Emily. 2018. "Launching a National Gun-Control Coalition, the Parkland Teens Meet Chicago's Young Activists." *The New Yorker,* June 26. Retrieved from https://www.newyorker.com/news/dispatch/launching-a-national-gun-control-coalition-the-parkland-teens-meet-chicagos-young-activists.

Wittgenstein, Ludwig. 2001. *Philosophical Investigations.* Oxford: Blackwell Publishing.

Wylie, Alison and Sergio Sismondo. 2015. "Standpoint Theory, In Science." In *International Encyclopedia of the Social and Behavioral Sciences,* edited by James D. Wright [Digital Edition]. Amsterdam: Elsevier.

Wylie, Alison. 2012. "Feminist Philosophy of Science: Standpoint Matters." *Proceedings and Addresses of the American Philosophical Association* 86 (2): 47–76.

Wylie, Alison. 1993. "Why Standpoint Matters." In *Science and Other Cultures: Issues in Philosophies of Science and Technology,* edited by Robert Figueroa and Sandra Harding, 26–48. New York: Routledge.

Index

contextualism, 107–8
Cook, Helen Appo, xi
Cooper, Anna Julia, xi
Cooper, Brittany, 34
Cornell University, 47–48
Cullors, Patrisse, ix, 86

Daniell, F. Raymond, 9
Daniels, Josephus, 10
De Dreu, Carsten, 17
Diagnostic and Statistical Manual of Mental Disorders (DSM-III), 51
DiAngelo, Robin, 63–65
disagreement (doxastic), 69–73;
  between asymmetrical social powers, 73
  as beneficial process, 71
  failures of, 97
  testimonial scenarios, 71–73
Doan, Michael, xxii, 112–14, 120
dominant knowers:
  and epistemic charity, 101
  and epistemic virtue, xvi–xvii
  identities of, xxiii
  and objectification of others, xiv
  rejection of marginalized perceptions, 42–43
  remediation of testimonial injustice, 2
  self-reflection, 120
Dotson, Kristie, xxiv, 26–27
double bind, 35
double-consciousness, x, xi, 102, 120
double-knowing:
  awareness of prejudice, xvii
  as epistemic labor, 23
  as epistemic stress response, xv–xvi
  practice of, 21
  relation to epistemic injustice, xii
  "seeing as," 23
  as survival strategy, 102
  and W.E.B. Du Bois, x, xi
Du Bois, W.E.B., ix, x, xi, 120

Ellis, Manuel, ix

environments, educational, 61, 85
environments, epistemic:
  corrupt, 42
  hostile, xii, xix, 65, 117
  polluted, 15
  prejudicial, xvi, 14, 25
  racialized by willful ignorance, 62
  shared, 37
  unjust, xi, 57, 63
environments, social, xvi, 12, 63, 65, 66, 67, 70
environments, testimonial, 24–25
epistemic advantage, 108–11
epistemic allies, xxi
epistemic burden, 42–43
epistemic charity, 99–102;
  evolving epistemic frameworks, 71
  failure to address injustice, 101–2
  palliative in nature, 99–101
epistemic disavowal, 38–42;
  defined, xvii, 23, 24
  and epistemic dissonance, 38
  extracted speech, 39
  in Kalief Browder case, xvii–xviii, 38–39
  Unbelievable (Netflix series), 39–40
epistemic dissonance:
  defined, 23
  and epistemic labor, xvii
epistemic exploitation, 33, 34, 35
epistemic frameworks. *See* frameworks, epistemic
epistemic injustice:
  epistemic resistance to, 114
  forms of, xiii
  historical, correction for, xvi
  scope, xi–xii
  structural, 112–13
Epistemic Injustice: Power and the Ethics of Knowing, xi
epistemic labor, 24–38;
  active resistance to, 24–25, 34
  to avoid harm, 14–15
  and epistemic disavowal, 21
  and epistemic dissonance, xvii

vs. personhood, xiv
surrender of, 24
Sismondo, Sergio, 104
social allowance, 11
social inequality:
 and epistemic inequality, xv–xvi
 permitted by society, 102
social marginalization, x
social power:
 active vs. passive, 2
 bestowing epistemic power, 101–2
 vs. epistemic power, xi
 structural, 2–3
sociology of dominance, 63
The Souls of Black Folk, 120
speech:
 on behalf of marginalized, 92
 and context, x
 and prejudice, x
 unjustly extracted, 39
Spiers, Hugo, 16–17
standpoint theories:
 contextualism, 107–8
 epistemic advantaged
  standpoints, 108
 epistemic priority/privilege, 102, 103
 essentialism, 103–6
 inversion thesis, 106–7
 legitimizing standpoints, 108
 strong objectivity, 102
 and systems of power, 108–9
Steinem, Gloria, 49
stereotyping:
 double-knowing, x
 heuristic value of, 3, 16
 inhibition of testimonial virtue, 2
 negative, cognitive disposition
  toward, 16
 obstacle to fruitful
  disagreement, 73–74
 reducing activation of, 76–85
 subliminal reflexivity of, 19–20
Stowe, Harriet Beecher, 13
structural epistemic justice, 112–20;
 affirmative action, 116

collaborative transformative
 strategy, 115
Flint Water Crisis case, 112–13, 114
racial integration, 116
redistribution of social power, 112
targeted redress, 117–19

The Talented Mr. Ripley, 5, 8–9, 11–13
Terrell, Mary Church, xi
testimonial injustice:
 agential and structural power
  remedies, 6
 defined, xiii
 epistemic harm, 4
 ethical harm, 4
 in *To Kill a Mockingbird*, 3–4
 mitigating impacts of, xiv–xv
 reconceptualizing remedies, 21
 remediating, 2
 secondary harm, 4–5
testimonial justice:
 neutralizing negative
  prejudice, 13–14
 operating unidirectionally, 14
testimonial quieting, 26–27
testimonial smothering, 26–27
testimonial virtue:
 cognitive roadblocks, 2, 15–16
 as corrective to prejudice, 6–7
 operating unidirectionally, 15
Thompson, Ahmir (Questlove),
 29–30, 31–32
Thoreau, Henry David, 15
Title VII of the 1964 Civil Rights
 Act, 48–49
Trans Women of Color Collective, 90
Trolley Problem, 17–18
Truth, Sojourner, xi, xxiv

Unbelievable (Netflix series), 39–40
Uncle Tom's Cabin, 13
University College London (UCL), 16
University of Amsterdam, 17
U. S. Supreme Court, 10
Us/Them:

About the Author

Kamili Posey is an assistant professor of philosophy at the City University of New York, Kingsborough. Her research interests include social epistemology, feminist epistemology, and philosophy of race and gender. Her publications appear in *Transactions of the Charles S. Peirce Society, Public Philosophy Journal*, and the *Social Epistemology Review and Reply Collective*, where she also serves as the book editor.

www.ingramcontent.com/pod-product-compliance
Lightning Source LLC
Chambersburg PA
CBHW022321280326
41932CB00010B/1189